Living and Celebratir
Our Catholic Customs and Ti

The Lent–
Easter Book

Joan Marie Arbogast

Selected crafts contributed by Natividade Pereira Nascimento, FSP

Illustrated by Virginia Helen Richards, FSP, and D. Thomas Halpin, FSP

Photos by Mary Emmanuel Alves, FSP

Pauline
BOOKS & MEDIA
Boston

Library of Congress Cataloging-in-Publication Data

Arbogast, Joan Marie.
  The Lent-Easter book / Joan Marie Arbogast; illustrated by Virginia Helen Richards ;
        photos by Mary Emmanuel Alves.
      p. cm. — (Living and celebrating our Catholic customs and traditions)
    ISBN 0-8198-4515-9
    1. Lent. 2. Easter. I. Richards, Virginia Helen. II. Alves, Mary Emmanuel, 1945– III. Title. IV. Series.

BV85.A68 2005
  263'.92—dc22

2004015420

All Scripture quotations in this publication are from the *Contemporary English Version* copyright © 1991, 1992, 1995 by American Bible Society. Used by permission.

Excerpts from the English translation of *The Roman Missal* © 1973, International Committee on English in the Liturgy, Inc. (ICEL).

Excerpts from the English translation of *Rite of Penance* © 1974, ICEL. All rights reserved.

The following stories first appeared in *My Friend: The Catholic Magazine for Kids* and are used with permission of the authors and illustrators:

"Tough Call," by Sandra Humphrey, illustrated by Ray Morelli

"I, Javiera," by Diana Jenkins, illustrated by Linda Rzoska

"The Candy Challenge," by Diana Jenkins, illustrated by Steve Delmonte

"Dare You," by Clare Mishica, illustrated by Virginia Esquinaldo

"The Challenge," by Carol A. Grund, illustrated by Luanne Marten

"Sunday Dinner," by Diana Jenkins, illustrated by Jack Hughes

"Is Jesus Alive?" by Sandra Humphrey, illustrated by Virginia Esquinaldo

"Easter Bible Cookies," adapted by Maria Grace Dateno, FSP, photos by Emmanuel Alves, FSP; art by Virginia Helen Richards, FSP, and D. Thomas Halpin, FSP

Crafts by Natividade Pereira Nascimento, FSP, pages 20, 64, 65, 96, 97, 98, 112, 114, 124, 133, 134.

Published by Pauline Books & Media, 50 Saint Pauls Avenue, Boston, MA 02130-3491. www.pauline.org

Printed in the U.S.A.

Pauline Books & Media is the publishing house of the Daughters of St. Paul, an international congregation of women religious serving the Church with the communications media.

2 3 4 5 6 7 8 9   13 12 11 10 09

Contents

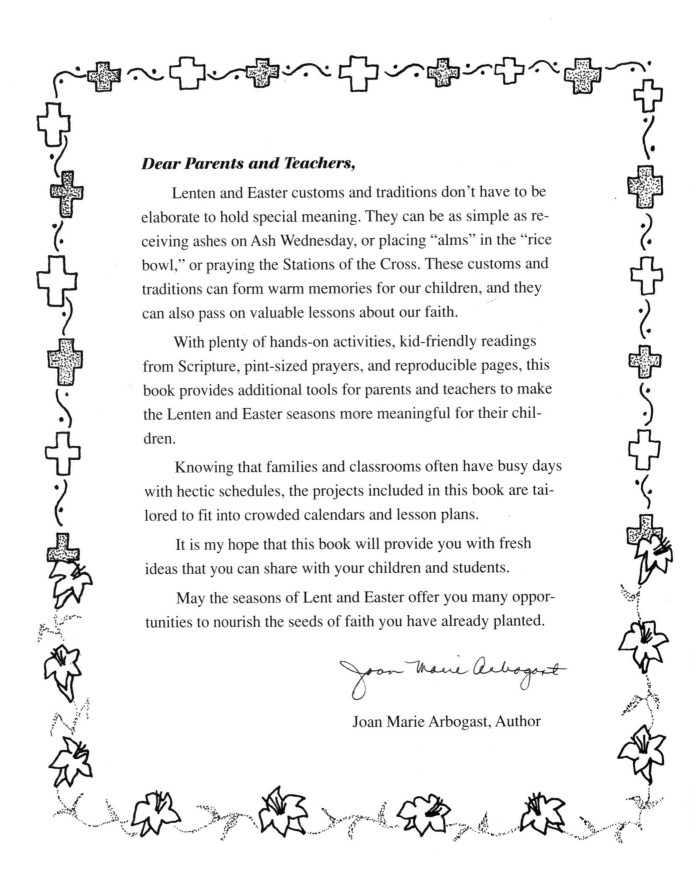

Dear Parents and Teachers,

Lenten and Easter customs and traditions don't have to be elaborate to hold special meaning. They can be as simple as receiving ashes on Ash Wednesday, or placing "alms" in the "rice bowl," or praying the Stations of the Cross. These customs and traditions can form warm memories for our children, and they can also pass on valuable lessons about our faith.

With plenty of hands-on activities, kid-friendly readings from Scripture, pint-sized prayers, and reproducible pages, this book provides additional tools for parents and teachers to make the Lenten and Easter seasons more meaningful for their children.

Knowing that families and classrooms often have busy days with hectic schedules, the projects included in this book are tailored to fit into crowded calendars and lesson plans.

It is my hope that this book will provide you with fresh ideas that you can share with your children and students.

May the seasons of Lent and Easter offer you many opportunities to nourish the seeds of faith you have already planted.

Joan Marie Arbogast, Author

How to Use This Book

The *Lent-Easter Book* is designed for use by teachers, DREs, parents, and anyone interested in passing on to children our faith traditions and symbols. It is versatile enough to be used with children at school or at home during the Lenten-Easter seasons. Lent begins on Ash Wednesday and ends on the evening of Holy Thursday with the Mass of the Lord's Supper. The Sacred Triduum begins with the Mass of the Lord's Supper and ends on the night of Holy Saturday at the Easter Vigil Mass. There is a chapter for each week of Lent, and one for Palm Sunday and Holy Week. The chapter for Easter includes the entire season, which lasts seven weeks—from Easter Sunday to Pentecost. It also includes several important feasts that we celebrate during the season: Divine Mercy Sunday, Good Shepherd Sunday, and the Ascension.

From the contents, you will see that the material for Lent is divided by **major themes of the season:** prayer; love and mercy; Reconciliation and peace; Baptism; the cross, death, and resurrection. If your religious education program is lectionary based, the beginning of each chapter indicates to which Sunday of Lent it corresponds.

The **reproducible section** (beginning on page 137) contains material that you can use throughout the Lenten-Easter season. Children can put together a reproducible guide for the sacrament of Reconciliation. Scenes from the Way of the Cross may be used as dramatized prayers, discussion starters, or class plays. Two versions of the Way of the Cross booklets (one for younger children, one for older children) are provided.

Every chapter begins with a **Week-at-a-Glance,** a handy tool for helping teachers and parents get an overview of the week's activities. Glancing through the week's activities ahead of time will alert you to any advance preparation that needs to be done. Each week includes a **story** from *My Friend: The Catholic Magazine for Kids,* **discussion starters** for both younger children and older children, **crafts** and **activities** related to the chapter's theme, **Family Take-Home Pages,** and **Family Customs and Traditions.**

The stories taken from *My Friend* can be read aloud to the children for discussion or left in a learning center for the children to read and to journal their reflections later. The stories may be photocopied for easier use in the classroom. In fact, any pages with a copyright symbol [©] at the bottom of the page may be photocopied. Simply make sure that the copyright symbol and reprint permission line are on the photocopy.

Each week of Lent begins with a Prayer Experience related to the theme for that particular week. The word "experience" is used because they vary in form, using traditional prayers, readings from Scripture, quiet reflections, and hands-on activities. Each "experience" ends with a two or three-line refrain for the week which can become part of your daily prayer routine.

Many of the craft and activity pages contain Bible verses related to the theme of the week, providing another opportunity to learn Scripture. Crafts and activities appropriate for younger children are marked "Easy." Some crafts have alternative directions for younger or older children. To make the templates for an activity a little sturdier, consider using card stock or cardboard. All activities can be adapted for the age of the children, so feel free to be creative with the suggestions given in this book to make them appropriate for your group.

You may want to keep handy some contemporary Christian music CDs—found at any Pauline Books & Media Center, Christian bookstore, or ordered off the internet—to use along with this book. Instrumental music is always useful for creating atmosphere. You will want to have a Bible on hand for many of the discussions with older students. A supplies list indicates what you will need for each craft or activity.

The Family Take-Home Pages in each chapter also strengthens the home-school connection. They provide information for parents and activities for families that support what children are learning in school. Send these pages home at the beginning of the week so that families have time to plan what evenings they will incorporate the suggested activities. The activities and prayer experiences on these pages are multi-age appropriate and are intended to be integrated over time.

The Family Customs and Traditions pages found at the end of each section will help families to rediscover the richness of es-

tablished family traditions and open the possibility of incorporating new customs into their Lenten and Easter observance.

Because Lent is traditionally the time of year when many adults are making the final preparations to enter the Church, some crafts and activities provide opportunities for children to encourage and welcome soon-to-be-members of the Church. Additional crafts and activities found in the Easter section encourage children to support the new members as they grow in faith.

Finally, because we want our children to live lives of faith, a variety of activities are included to encourage children to turn their faith into action.

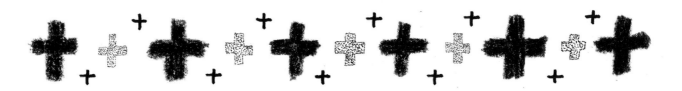

Ash Wednesday

Ash Wednesday marks the first day of Lent, our forty-day journey to Easter. During this solemn season, we recall "the great events that gave us life in Christ" in order that God might bring to perfection in us the image of his Son (cf. Preface for Lent I).

Lent calls us to prayerful reflection, to penance, fasting, and almsgiving. Lent leads us to the holiest week of the liturgical year and to the joyful celebration of Easter.

To set a reflective tone, use these simple Lenten symbols. Weave a purple ribbon around a grapevine wreath, and then place it on a table. Stand one white or purple candle in the center of the wreath and place three nails near it. The wreath and nails symbolize Christ's crucifixion; the purple ribbon, the season of Lent and our need for repentance; and the candle, Christ, our Savior and Light of the world.

Help your children recognize Ash Wednesday as a special day in the liturgical year with the following prayer service. Then celebrate the Eucharist and receive ashes together as a family or school community.

Ash Wednesday Prayer

Have one person light the Lenten candle, one read from Scripture, and one read the prayer.

Leader:

Dear Jesus, open our minds and hearts
that we might hear and follow your word.

*A reading from the Prophet Daniel
9:3–5, 17, 18*

Then, to show my sorrow, I went without eating and dressed in sackcloth and sat in ashes. I confessed my sins and earnestly prayed to the LORD my God: "Our LORD, you are a great and fearsome God, and you faithfully keep your agreement with those who love and obey you. But we have sinned terribly by rebelling against you and rejecting your laws and teachings…. I am your servant, LORD God, and I beg you to answer my prayers…. Please show mercy to your chosen city, not because we deserve it, but because of your great kindness."

Allow time for quiet reflection and then continue with prayer.

Leader:

Dear Jesus,
today is Ash Wednesday,
the first day of Lent.

It is the beginning
of our forty-day journey
to Easter with you.

Please help us to turn away from sin.
Heal our weakness and make us true
friends of God.

May our sacrifices, prayers,
and kindness to others
bring us closer to you each day.

May the ashes we receive today
be an outward sign of our faith
and our love for you.

All: Amen.

Ash Wednesday

Dear Parent(s),

During this Lenten season, we will be focusing on the many different aspects of Lent: its meaning, its symbols, its customs, and its traditions. Each week your child will bring home Family Take-Home Pages, which will be filled with suggested activities that reinforce what we are discussing and learning in class. With the exception of this first one, these Take-Home Pages will be theme based and divided into three sections: Warm-Up Exercises, Getting Started, and Putting It into Practice.

To help create a reflective Lenten atmosphere to your home, consider using a simple Lenten candle. Take a purple pillar candle and place it in a candle dish. You can place three large nails at the base of the candle. Each night, your family can light the Lenten candle and say together the prayer on the Family Take-Home pages.

The Take-Home Pages for this week cover basic questions and answers about Lenten customs and symbols, and a prayer to share with your family on Ash Wednesday, the first day of Lent.

Questions Kids Ask About Lent

Why are we marked with ashes on Ash Wednesday?

In Biblical days, people wore sackcloth and sat in ashes as a sign of penance. Today we receive ashes on Ash Wednesday because it is the beginning of Lent, our season of repentance. When we receive the blessed ashes on our forehead, we hear the words, "Turn from sin and be faithful to the Gospel," or, "Remember that you are dust and unto dust you shall return." Ashes remind us that we are sinners and that we must turn from our sins and grow closer to God.

Where do the ashes come from?

The ashes we receive on our foreheads come from the burnt palms from the previous year's Palm Sunday.

Why are the vestments purple during Lent?

Purple reminds us that Lent is a time of serious commitment to penance and prayerful reflection. It was also a color worn by kings during ancient times. So it makes sense that the color we associate with Lent would be purple, because during this time we focus on the life of Jesus, the King of kings.

Why does Lent last for forty days?

The Bible uses the number forty repeatedly. The great flood that kept Noah and his family afloat lasted for forty days and forty nights. After fleeing Egypt, the Israelites wandered for forty years in the desert before they entered the Promised Land. Jesus spent forty days and forty nights in the desert preparing for his public ministry. These forty-day or forty-year periods included times of great trials and difficulties, times of searching, reflection, and action. We are also called to reflect on our faith, to search our hearts, and to change our ways during our forty days of Lent.

Why do we say there are forty days of Lent when, according to the calendar, there are more than forty days?

Lent seems longer than forty days, but it actually isn't. Lent begins on Ash Wednesday and ends the evening of Holy Thursday. We don't count Sundays as days of Lent, because we celebrate Christ's Resurrection every Sunday at Mass—that makes Sundays like mini-Easters! So if you count the days starting with Ash Wednesday, skipping Sundays, and ending on Holy Thursday, you'll discover that Lent is exactly forty days.

Why do we "give up" things during Lent?

Lent is a time to be renewed in spirit. The discipline we practice through "giving things up" helps us to control our desires and to grow in our longing for all that is true, good, and beautiful. Voluntary self-denial helps us think of God; it also helps us think of others, too. How? Let's say you give up candy during Lent. By doing so, you save money. Rather than keep the money for yourself, you can give it to charity. Instead of giving something up, some people choose to do something extra, for example, pray a Rosary or help a neighbor in need.

Why do Catholics give up meat on Fridays of Lent?

Lent is an intense season of the Church's penitential practice. Catholics who are 14 years or older do not eat meat on Ash Wednesday, Good Friday, and all other Fridays during Lent. The Church asks all Catholics to make this obligatory penance a part of their Lenten program of self-denial.

Why can't adults eat between meals on Ash Wednesday and Good Friday?

This is another special sacrifice that Catholics between the ages of 18 and 59 are asked to make. It's called fasting. It means that on these days, Catholics can eat one full meal, plus two light meals that together don't equal a meal, and they can't eat snacks in between. Those younger than 18 are not expected to "fast" from food, but they can "fast" from or give up other things such as sweets, insisting on their own way, or arguing with a sibling or a parent.

Why don't we sing or say "alleluia" during Lent?

The word alleluia, or "hallelu-yah" is of Hebrew origin, meaning "praise God." It is associated with joy and festivity. We "put away" all alleluias during Lent as we reflect on the last days of Jesus' life, and his crucifixion and death. During the Easter season, we sing and pray many alleluias as we celebrate our new life in Christ, our Savior and Lord.

Ash Wednesday Prayer

Jesus,
today is Ash Wednesday,
the first day of Lent.
Blessed ashes mark our faith.
They call us to repentance.
Pardon our sins, O Jesus.
We are sorry for sometimes
choosing not to follow your way.
Please help us start over.
Please help us begin today.
May this season of Lent bring us closer
to you, our Amazing Grace.
May we grow stronger in
our commitment
to follow you more closely, day after day.
Amen.

Together as a family or school community attend Mass on Ash Wednesday and receive ashes as a sign of your willingness to grow closer to Christ during this Lenten season.

Prayer

Each week during the Lenten and Easter seasons, we will be focusing on a different theme. The theme for this week of Lent is Prayer.

It is important that our children understand that there are many forms of prayer and that all forms of prayer can lead to a closer relationship with God.

A variety of prayer activities is provided, so you can choose those that best fit your children's needs. Some of the activities call for quiet reflection and some require advance planning because you will need to gather supplies and assemble a simple project that will be used by children during the week or perhaps the entire Lenten season.

For those following a lectionary-based catechesis, this theme corresponds to the readings for the first Sunday of Lent.

Week-at-a-Glance

Supplies needed:

prayer table with Lenten candle

Gather everyone around the prayer table and light the Lenten candle.

Say to the children: Lent is a special time during the liturgical year when we examine how well we are living our faith. Are we following in Jesus' footsteps? Are we growing closer to him with each passing day?

Prayer can help us grow closer to Jesus. Prayer is simply a conversation with God. We can speak to God aloud or in our hearts. We can even write our thoughts to God or sing a song. When we finish talking, we need to listen for God's response. So let's practice listening now.

A reading from first Samuel 3:1–10

Samuel served the LORD by helping Eli the priest, who was by that time almost blind. In those days, the LORD hardly ever spoke directly to people, and he did not appear to them in dreams very often. But one night, Eli was asleep in his room, and Samuel was sleeping on a mat near the sacred chest in the LORD's house. They had not been asleep very long when the LORD called out Samuel's name. "Here I am."

"I didn't call you," Eli answered. "Go back to bed." Samuel went back.

Again the LORD called out Samuel's name. Samuel got up and went to Eli. "Here I am," he said. "What do you want?"

Eli told him, "Son, I didn't call you. Go back to sleep."

The LORD had not spoken to Samuel before, and Samuel did not recognize the voice. When the LORD called out his name for the third time, Samuel went to Eli again and said, "Here I am. What do you want?"

Eli finally realized that it was the LORD who was speaking to Samuel. So he said, "Go back and lie down! If someone speaks to you again, answer, 'I'm listening, LORD. What do you want me to do?'"

Once again Samuel went back and lay down.

The LORD then stood beside Samuel and called out as he had done before, "Samuel! Samuel!"

"I'm listening," Samuel answered. "What do you want me to do?"

After God got Samuel's attention, he told Samuel what he wanted him to do.

Now let's take a few moments to ask God what he wants us to do. Close your eyes. Sit quietly. Ask God to help you know what he wants you to do. Then be patient and listen. In the silence, God will speak to your heart so you will know what it is he wants you to do. (Allow a few minutes for quiet reflection and then close with this short prayer.)

Closing Prayer

Speak Lord. I'm listening,
I'm listening to you.
What is it that you want me to do?

To encourage your children to "listen" for God's direction in their lives, pray this prayer often throughout the week. (You may want to write it on the chalkboard at school or on an index card that you can place on your prayer table at home where it will serve as a visible reminder.)

Tough Call

By Sandra Humphrey and illustrated by Ray Morelli

O nly Eric could strike out three times in a row and still smile. No wonder all the guys called him a dork. I sneaked a quick peek at the bleachers. Eddie was doing his finger-across-the-throat thing and Frankie was covering his eyes as if he couldn't stand to watch any more of the game.

Instead of going back to the dugout and sitting with the guys, after he struck out, Eric began picking up empty pop cans and tossing them in the recycling bin. He's always doing stuff like that. It's like he thinks he's on a personal mission to save the earth.

As usual, our team, the Wildcats, lost and I watched Eric amble off toward home, still picking up litter.

As I headed to the locker room, I had no idea that my world as I knew it was about to crash and burn.

My friends were already there waiting for me. Andy was laughing so hard, he was just about doubled over, holding his stomach.

"So is this a great idea or is this a great idea?" he finally managed to sputter, while he leaned against his locker to keep from falling over.

Kevin slapped him on the back and grinned. "You're a genius, man. Maybe not in math, but this is a seriously brilliant idea."

Leon gave him a thumbs-up. "Totally cool, bro."

If it was Andy's idea, I knew someone was going to get hurt and all my sensors were sounding a red alert. But I asked anyway. "So what's going on?"

Andy was off on another laughing binge, so Kevin tried to explain.

"You know how Eric invited the four of us to his birthday party next Saturday?"

Then Leon screwed up his face and mimicked Eric's scratchy voice. "'Do you think that maybe if you're not doing anything else you might be able to come over to my house on Saturday to help me celebrate my birthday? That is, if you're not already doing something else?'"

Then Kevin took over again. "So Andy comes up with

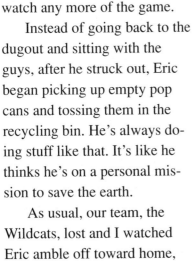

this really brilliant idea. We're all going to tell Eric we're coming to his party and then none of us are going to show up. Let's roll the video: I can see Eric now. He's pacing back and forth wondering where everyone is. It's getting later and later and still no one shows up."

While Kevin was rolling his imaginary video, Andy grabbed his throat with both hands. Then he stuck out his tongue and looked cross-eyed. "And then maybe he'll finally get it. We don't want to be his friends. So when are we going to be his friends? Never. That's when. When are we going to be his friends?"

The other guys echoed, "Never, that's when."

I could feel my face heating up. I knew this was wrong, but I felt helpless.

Kevin pounded me on the back and shot me a grin. "So are you with us?"

I didn't know what else to do, so I just shrugged, which I guess he took for a yes. Boy, did I feel sick to my stomach. Like I was going to throw up.

As we headed home, the guys were still making plans for Saturday. Roller blading and pizza and no Eric.

That night I plopped down on my bed and stared at the water spots on my ceiling. That's how I relax. Some kids listen to rock or rap, but I relax by staring at the water spots on my

ceiling. It's kind of like staring at the clouds in the sky.

Right now, I could see a bear and a butterfly, or maybe it was a bat. And what looked like part of a guitar. Finally, I couldn't avoid the inevitable any longer. I had to do some serious thinking about Eric.

Eric and his jeans. The jeans were too short for him, the jeans with holes. *Real* holes, not holes like the rest of us made in our jeans to look cool.

Eric who's so quiet that sometimes I wonder if his lips are stuck together with Velcro. And when he does talk, he talks about how fossil fuels can

cause global warming, while the rest of us are talking baseball and football scores. Besides, Eric's new this year and nobody likes new.

I could feel my stomach twisting into a knot. This was a dark day and getting darker by the second. It looked like this was going to be one of those no-win situations. If I joined the other guys and boycotted Eric's party, I knew I would feel rotten.

But if I did show up at Eric's party, that would be the

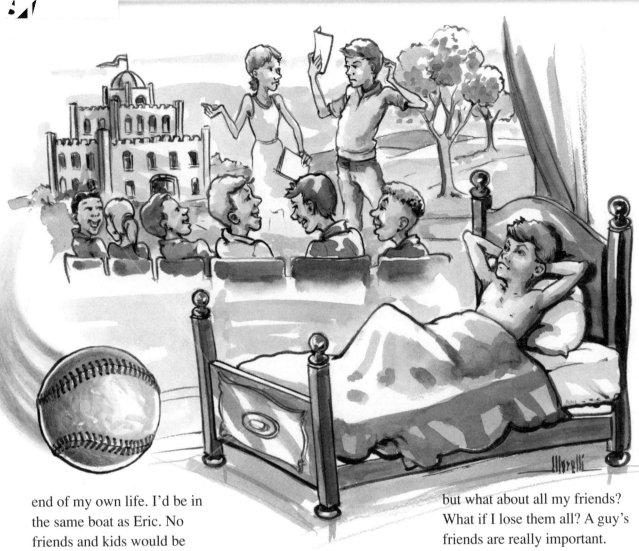

end of my own life. I'd be in the same boat as Eric. No friends and kids would be laughing at me behind *my* back.

I know what it's like to have kids laughing at you. That memory is burned into my memory bank forever. Last year my friend Eddie persuaded me to try out for the class play and, against my better judgment, I did. I can still see myself standing alone up there on that huge stage—my face neon red, my knees turning to Jell-O, and my mouth so dry it felt like I'd swallowed my pillow. And I couldn't even read my script because my hand was shaking so badly. The words just looked like a bunch of Egyptian hieroglyphics.

The other kids were practically rolling in the aisles—they were laughing so hard. Eddie ended up getting a part in the play and I ended up painting scenery.

So what was I going to do about Eric? God, I think I need some help here. I know what Jesus would do. If he promised to do something, he would do it. And I said I would go to the party, so I know I should go, but what about all my friends? What if I lose them all? A guy's friends are really important.

I think this is one of those tough choices where you know what is right, but it's still hard to do it. I'd still have my friends in my youth group at church, so I guess it's not like I'd be losing all my friends.

Boy, God, this has been a really tough call, but I know what I have to do. I think I'll give Eric a call and see if he wants anything special for his birthday.

And, God? Thanks for listening and always being there for me.

Reprinted from My Friend: The Catholic Magazine for Kids, *Pauline Books & Media, 50 Saint Pauls Avenue, Boston, MA 02130.* www.myfriendmagazine.com

The Lent–Easter Book

Discussion Starters for Grades K–3

Think of a time when you had to make a tough decision like the one in this story.

- How did you know what you should do?

- Did you ask Jesus to help you? Why or why not?

- How can prayer help us make good decisions?

Discussion Starters for Grades 4–8

Think of a time when you knew that you should have done something nice for someone else, but you didn't really want to do it.

- What did you finally decide to do? Why?

- Did you specifically ask God to help you? How did prayer help?

- If you didn't actually say a prayer, was there some other quiet urging or voice, for example a verse from the Bible, that helped you come to your decision? If so, the Holy Spirit and the Word of God led you, and that's totally awesome!

- How did the decision you made affect the other person? How did it affect you?

- If you had it to do over again, would you do the same thing or would you respond differently? Why?

Everyone has embarrassing moments. Recall one of yours. What happened?

- Were others around? How did they react? And how did that make you feel?

- Did anyone come to your rescue? What did he/she say or do?

- How did that simple act of kindness make you feel?

- At any time during that whole incident, did you turn to God in prayer?

- If so, when did you pray? What did you say? How did prayer help?

- If that same situation happened today to someone else, how would you react and why?

Now suppose you have a really tough decision to make, and there are no easy answers.

- Who do you turn to for help? Your friends? Your parents? Another trusted adult?

- Do you turn to God? Why? Why not?

- What are the advantages of turning to each of these different sources for help?

- Have you ever asked a friend or your parents to pray for you when you've had a tough decision to make? Why, why not?

Have the children write a letter to God starting with these words: "God, there are so many areas in my life in which I want to grow. I want to trust you with my life. I want to believe that you care about what is going on in my life. I need help forgiving others and need help with my temper. I wish I could accept myself, but often I can't. I sometimes give in to the temptations in my life. Please help me, Jesus, to grow in…." Have the children seal their letters in an envelope and place them on the prayer table. As class starts each day, gather at the prayer table and pray together.

Prayer Rock

Easy

This craft is perfect for younger children. This decorative rock can help children remember to say their morning and night prayers because they can keep it right next to their beds!

Supplies needed:

smooth, rounded rock or stone (1 per child; the rock should fit comfortably in a child's hand)

acrylic paints* (varied colors)

small paper plates or plastic containers

paintbrushes

paint shirts or smocks

newspaper

Directions:

1. Have children spread newspaper over work surfaces and put on their paint shirts.

2. Ask every child to choose a small rock or large stone for this project. It should be washed to remove loose dirt and debris (if this is a school project, have students wash the rocks at home).

3. Pour paints onto paper plates or into plastic containers.

4. When the rocks are dry, paint them with colorful crosses or with phrases such as "Prayer Rock!" framed with colorful borders. They should paint one side and then let it dry on newspaper. After it dries, have students personalize the other side, too.

Whenever working with paints, have children spread newspaper on work surfaces and wear paint shirts, smocks, or other protective clothing.

5. Once prayer rocks are finished, have children hold their prayer rocks in their hands while you pray this simple prayer:

Dear God,
please bless these rocks we have painted.
We will be placing them next to our beds
so they will remind us to praise you
when we wake in the morning
and to thank you when we go to sleep at night.
We know we can pray anytime and any place
but we want to make sure we begin
and end our days talking with you.
Thank you for always listening.
Thank you for the gift of prayer.
Amen.

The Lent–Easter Book

Prayer Journal

This personalized prayer journal is the perfect place for children* to write down some of their conversations with God. Whether used daily or weekly throughout the rest of the school year, this journal will record your children's words of praise, thanksgiving, petition, and sorrow.

In addition to this activity, you might even consider having your younger and older children pair up as prayer partners during the season of Lent. Each could pray for the other in the weeks ahead!

Supplies needed:

spiral-bound notebook (1 per child)

scissors

magazines/newspapers

glue stick

clear contact paper 8 1/2" by 11"
(2 sheets per child)

Directions:

1. Have children leaf through old magazines and newspapers to find pictures, words, or phrases that illustrate a variety of things for which they are thankful. Clip these items from the magazines and newspapers.

2. Form a collage with these items by placing them—but not yet gluing them—onto the front covers of their notebooks.

3. After determining the layout of collages, glue pieces into place. Repeat this process for the back cover.

4. Cover the front and back of collage-covered notebooks with contact paper. These pieces should measure 2 inches longer and 1 inch wider than their notebooks; the excess will be folded inside the covers.

5. Place the contact paper over the front cover of notebooks, lining the contact paper up to but not onto the spiral binding. The contact paper should extend 1 inch beyond the edges of the cover not bound by the spiral. Cut off the corners of the contact paper before folding the excess to the inside of the front cover.

6. Repeat the same process for the back cover.

_____

Younger children will need help with this project. You can buddy-up older children with younger ones. Not only can the older children help the younger ones make their journals, they can also help record their prayers. (You may decide to have younger children "draw" rather than write their prayers.)

Prayer Starters for Prayer Journals

Explain to your children that prayer comes in all shapes and sizes. It can be in the form of traditional prayers like the Our Father, Hail Mary, and Glory, or it can be as simple as, "Thank you, God!" Prayer can be spoken, thought, or written. It can be silent or sung. Prayer can be private or communal. It can be short or ramble on. God simply wants us to come to him in prayer–always, anytime, anywhere. This activity will also help children learn the five (types/ends) of prayer.

Directions:

1. To help children think about their conversations with God, have them recall some recent conversations with their friends.*

2. On the chalkboard, list the topics they discussed, how they felt, how they think their friends felt, and why they like to be with their friends.

3. Introduce prayer as a conversation with God, who is also our Friend.

4. Discuss some of the things they may have talked with God about in the past. How did they feel? How do they think God felt?

5. Continue by having the students select five "prayer starters" from the list provided, or have them come up with some of their own if they prefer.

6. Then have them write personal prayers of praise, thanks, adoration, petition, and intercession in their prayer journals.

7. Finally, have them choose one of the prayers to share with the group.

---

* This makes a perfect "buddy project" for pairing up older children with younger ones. The younger children can draw their prayers while the older children can write the "prayer starters" across the top of the pages.

Prayer Starters

Good morning, Jesus! Thank you for…

Heavenly Father, I think it's awesome that…

Dear God, I'm so sorry that I…

Oh, Jesus, I did it again! I…

Dear Jesus, please bless my friend who needs your help with…

Dearest Jesus, I know that you love me because…

Abba, Father, I'm worried about…

Sweet Jesus, please help me to…

Thank you, dear Jesus, for…

Our Father, I know you understand how I feel about…

Dear God, I'm so happy I could…

Holy Spirit, I have a tough decision to make about…

Don't forget. You can also ask the Blessed Mother, St. Joseph, and all the angels and saints to pray to God for you and your needs.

Prayer Jar

Easy

This activity reminds children to pray more often during Lent so that prayer becomes a part of daily routine as we move into the Easter season.

Teacher/Parent preparation:

You will need to make the prayer jar in advance. See directions below.

Supplies needed:

1 large plastic jar per class or family (gallon-size or smaller)

construction paper: purple, pink, green, yellow, blue, white

measuring tape

pencil

scissors

glue

marker

6 plastic baggies

double-sided tape or clear-drying craft glue

Make a large sign saying: We can pray in all sorts of ways! Purple = prayer of intercession; pink = prayer of praise; green = prayer of thanks; yellow = prayer of petition; blue = prayer of adoration; white = a combination of prayers.

Directions for making prayer jar:

1. Wash, rinse, and dry empty jar.
2. Measure the circumference of the jar. Then cut a 2-inch-wide strip of construction paper the length of the circumference.
3. On the "label," print the words, GROWING IN PRAYER, with a marker. The letters should "grow" from tiny letters to large letters as shown here: GROWING IN PRAYER.

4. Tape or glue the "label" onto the jar.
5. Cut the 6 different colors of construction paper into small strips measuring 1/2 inch wide by 3 inches long. Place strips into plastic baggies for later use. Each baggie holds a different color. Label each bag with the type of prayer and the color.

Directions for activity:

For Older Children

Whenever a child prays privately, he/she places a color-coded slip of paper into the jar. This activity helps children to realize how often they turn to God in need, in thanksgiving, in praise, in adoration, and in intercession.

For Younger Children

Every time a child prays privately, he/she places a strip of paper—any color—into the jar. By Easter, the jar should be overflowing.

Making Pretzels

Kitchen fun can provide teachable moments.* So roll up your sleeves and help your children learn how traditional pretzels can remind us of God.

Ingredients:

1 1/2 cups warm water
1 pkg. active dry yeast
1/2 tsp. sugar
1/2 tsp. salt
4 1/2–5 cups unsifted flour
1 egg, beaten (for glazing pretzels)
coarse salt (to sprinkle on glaze)

Directions:

1. In a large bowl, dissolve yeast according to the directions on the package.

2. Add sugar and salt; stir until dissolved.

3. Add 3 cups of flour, stirring until all flour is mixed.

4. Add remaining flour and knead dough until smooth.

5. Place dough back in bowl, cover with a towel, and let dough rest for an hour or more.

6. Give each child a golf-ball size piece of dough. Have them roll the dough in the palms of their hands until they have 12-inch long strips.

7. Form pretzels on greased cookie sheet. Brush pretzels with beaten egg and sprinkle with coarse salt.

8. Bake at 425 degrees for 12–15 minutes. Makes 2 dozen pretzels.

---

* As you're mixing the ingredients and kneading the dough, talk about the shape of a traditional pretzel. It has three parts to the whole, making it a perfect discussion-starter for talking about the Trinity: God the Father, God the Son, God the Holy Spirit. Its shape can also remind us of arms crossed over the chest, which is how early Christians prayed. Rather than folding their hands as we often do, they crossed their arms over their hearts. Monks are credited with forming these traditional pretzels as symbols of arms crossed in prayer.

Reflection

Redeemer of the world, give us a greater share of your passion through a deeper spirit of repentance, so that we may share the glory of your resurrection.

The Liturgy

Prayer

Dear Parent(s),

During the Lenten season, we will be focusing on different aspects of Lent: its meaning, its symbols, its customs, and its traditions. Each week, your child will bring home Family Take-Home Pages, which are filled with activities that reinforce what we are discussing and learning in class. These Take-Home Pages are theme based and divided into three sections: Warm-Up Exercises, Getting Started, and Putting It into Practice. The theme for this week of Lent is Prayer. May the activities suggested in these pages provide you with additional tools for nurturing your child's faith.

Warm-Up Exercises...

Gather the family around the Lenten candle. Have one member of the family light the candle and another read from Scripture.

A reading from Luke 4:1–13

When Jesus returned from the Jordan River, the power of the Holy Spirit was with him, and the Spirit led him into the desert. For forty days Jesus was tested by the devil, and during that time he went without eating. When it was all over, he was hungry. The devil said to Jesus, "If you are God's Son, tell this stone to turn into bread."

Jesus answered, "The Scriptures say, 'No one can live only on food.'"

Then the devil led Jesus up to a high place and quickly showed him all the nations on earth. The devil said, "I will give all this power and glory to you. It has been given to me, and I can give it to anyone I want to. Just worship me, and you can have it all."

Jesus answered, "The Scriptures say: 'Worship the Lord your God and serve only him!'"

Finally, the devil took Jesus to Jerusalem and had him stand on top of the temple. The devil said, "If you are God's Son, jump off. The Scriptures say: 'God will tell his angels to take care of you. They will catch you in their arms, and you will not hurt your feet on the stones.'"

Jesus answered, "The Scriptures also say, 'Don't try to test the Lord your God!'"

After the devil had finished testing Jesus in every way possible, he left him for a while.

After sharing this passage with your family, lead them in a discussion. You may want to use the following questions:

We heard how the devil tried to tempt Jesus. How do you think the devil tempts us today?

What are some of the things that keep us from spending time with Jesus? Could these be temptations, too?

How can temptations be harmful?

What can we do to avoid temptation?

How can prayer help us avoid temptation?

How often do we turn to Jesus in prayer?

Follow your discussion with prayer. Have everyone close their eyes. Then tell them: Everyone struggles with temptations. Sometimes it's not easy to do what is right. Think about something you're struggling with now. Is it like a boxing match? A wrestling match? A dark cloud? Drowning? Now picture Jesus right there with you in the struggle. Put the struggle or the temptation right at Jesus' feet. You go to a river and sit on the riverbank. Jesus tells you he understands your struggles. He also had to struggle. Tell Jesus everything in your heart. Feel Jesus put his arm on your shoulder. No matter how many times you may have fallen, Jesus still puts his arm on your shoulder and says, "I died that you might live for me and be truly happy. I will never leave you. You mean so much to me that I gave up my life in order to save you. Count on me to be there with you all the time. I am always there to help you."

After the prayer, talk briefly about what it is like to know that Jesus understands. Come up with a prayer you can pray as a family in tough situations, such as, "God bless you, God love you, God keep you," or, "Jesus, I'm so weak, help me." Suggest these words to each other when things are tough.

Then pray the Our Father together as a family.

Getting Started...

The Bible gives us lots of clues about praying. In the Gospel of Matthew (6:6), we discover that Jesus told his followers, "When you pray, go into a room alone and close the door. Pray to your Father in private. He knows what is done in private, and he will reward you."

Jesus wasn't talking about going to your bedroom to pray. He was talking about the "inner room" of your heart. When you block everything from your mind except for Jesus, then you will find that "inner room." Even in a room full of people, you can pray privately in your heart.

Help your children learn to find that "inner room" with the following exercise.

Have your children find a comfortable place to sit and have them close their eyes. Tell them: Imagine a breeze blowing you far, far away. Toss your worries from your mind.

Let the wind carry them away. Pause, then add: Now, relax and think of Jesus. Repeat silently, Jesus, I love you. Jesus, I love you. Say it over and over again. Once you've focused on Jesus, sit quietly with him.

After a few minutes, have the children open their eyes. Explain that this is called meditation.

Putting It into Practice...

The Bible tells us to "Pray without ceasing" (1 Thessalonians 5:17). Why not make this your family's goal for this week?

Here are some suggestions to get you started:

Whenever you hear an ambulance siren, pray for the person in need of medical attention, medical personnel, and family members.

Whenever someone tells you wonderful news, thank God for that blessing.

Whenever you hear bad news, say a prayer for the person(s) involved.

When a friend or neighbor is going through a difficult time, pray for him or her.

When you receive a card, letter, or e-mail, pray for the person who sent it.

When someone celebrates a birthday, sing: May the dear Lord bless you... (to the same tune as Happy Birthday). Song is prayer, too!

See how many suggestions your family can come up with. Happy praying!

Praying the Rosary

The Rosary is a Gospel prayer in which we contemplate the lives of Jesus and Mary. In the Rosary, we pray with Mary to grow closer to her Son, Jesus.

Often a parent will "lead" the first half of the Our Father, Hail Mary, and Glory, while the children join in with the second half. But you may want to let your children "lead" different decades of the Rosary. (You can obtain posters of the mysteries of the Rosary at www.pauline.org.)

Though the joyful, sorrowful, and glorious mysteries have been around for centuries, Pope John Paul II added another set of mysteries in 2002—the luminous mysteries. Some families prefer to meditate on the sorrowful mysteries during Lent. Other families prefer to use the luminous mysteries during the first five weeks of Lent and the sorrowful mysteries during Holy Week. During the Easter season, the glorious mysteries are preferred.

How to Pray the Rosary

1. Start by making the Sign of the Cross.
2. Pray the Apostles' Creed, then one Our Father, three Hail Marys, and one Glory.
3. Announce the first mystery (see mysteries following.) Explain it to your children or read it from the Bible, and then pray a decade of the Rosary, which includes one Our Father, ten Hail Marys, and one Glory.
4. Announce the second mystery and then pray one Our Father, ten Hail Marys, and one Glory.
5. Repeat this process, announcing a different mystery with each decade.
6. When all five mysteries are completed, pray the Hail, Holy Queen.

Mysteries of the Rosary

Joyful Mysteries

The Angel announces to Mary she is to be the Mother of God's Son (Lk 1:26–29, 38); Mary visits Elizabeth (Lk 1:40–42); Jesus is born (Lk 2:6–7); Jesus is presented in the Temple (Lk 2:22, 34, 35); the finding of the child Jesus in the Temple (Lk 2:42–43, 46).

Luminous Mysteries

John baptizes Jesus (Mt 3:16–17); Jesus reveals his glory at the wedding at Cana (Jn 2:1–5, 9–11); Jesus proclaims the Kingdom of God (Mt 1:14–15); Jesus is transfigured (Mt 9:2–3, 7); Jesus gives us the Eucharist (Mt 14:22–25).

Sorrowful Mysteries

Jesus prays in the Garden of Gethsemane (Mk 14:32, 35–36); Jesus is scourged (Mt 27:26); Jesus is crowned with thorns (Mt 27:28–30); Jesus carries the cross (Jn 19:17); Jesus is crucified (Jn 19:25–27).

Glorious Mysteries

Jesus rises from the dead (Lk 24:1, 4–7); Jesus ascends into heaven (Acts 1:9–11); the Holy Spirit descends upon the Apostles (Acts 2:1–4); Mary is assumed into heaven (Jn 14:3); Mary is crowned Queen of heaven and earth (Rev 12:1).

Love and Mercy

Each week during the Lenten and Easter seasons, we will be focusing on a different theme. The theme for this week of Lent is Love and Mercy.

A variety of activities is provided so you can choose those that best fit your children's needs. Some activities call for quiet reflection and others involve group discussions. Some require advance planning because you will need to gather supplies for craft projects. You may want to flip to the back of the book to the reproducible pages to see if there are any additional materials you might want to use.

Lent is a time of serious reflection. It is a time when we examine how well we are living our faith. It is important that children understand that love leads us to action, and acts of mercy reflect God's love.

For those following a lectionary-based catechesis, this theme corresponds to the readings for the fifth Sunday of Lent.

Week-at-a-Glance

Supplies needed:

- gift basket (lined with purple tissue paper)
- cellophane (to wrap gift basket)
- ribbon   1 gift tag
- blank paper (1 per child)
- crayons, markers, or colored pencils

Gather everyone around the prayer table with the gift basket on it. Light the Lenten candle (see page 11).

Say to the children: Lent is a special time in the Church year when we examine how well we are following Jesus. Are we sharing God's love and mercy with others the way Jesus would? Holy Scripture teaches us how to live our faith. So, close your eyes and listen carefully to these words from Scripture.

A reading from the letter of James 2:14–17

My friends, what good is it to say you have faith, when you don't do anything to show that you really do have faith? Can that kind of faith save you? If you know someone who doesn't have any clothes or food, you shouldn't just say, "I hope all goes well for you. I hope you will be warm and have plenty to eat." What good is it to say this, unless you do something to help? Faith that doesn't lead us to do good deeds is all alone and dead!

Ask the children to keep their eyes closed while they think about the following questions: How have others helped you? What do you feel like when someone helps you? How do you help someone you know? What else could you do? How can you help that person this week?

After the children decide what they will do for someone else, they can open their eyes, get a piece of paper, and return to their seats. Have them draw a gift box on one side of the paper, and on the other side write or draw their gift for Jesus—what they plan to do for the other person.

Decorate the "packages" with markers, crayons, or colored pencils before placing them in the gift basket on the prayer table.

Everyone should remain silent while waiting for each person to place his/her "gift(s)" in the basket.

Once all "gifts" are in the basket, wrap it with cellophane, secure it with a ribbon, and attach a gift tag that reads: Our Gifts of Love and Mercy.

Keep the basket on the prayer table as a reminder of the good deeds that will be shared this week.

Gather around the prayer table.*

Closing Prayer for Younger Children

I love you with all my heart, dear God.
Please help me to love others, too.

Closing Prayer for Older Children

Father of Love and Mercy,
I want to mirror your mercy and love.

---

* Note: Use this prayer throughout the week with your children to remind them of their commitment to acts of mercy and love. Either prayer could easily be incorporated into morning prayer, grace before meals, or the afternoon prayer before dismissal from school. For home use, it could be added to morning or bedtime prayer routines or with grace before meals.

Love and Mercy

I, Javiera

By Diana R. Jenkins and illustrated by Linda Rzoska

"Hey, Javiera! Isn't that your uncle?"

I looked where Dani was pointing. Uncle Sergio was parked behind the school buses. He honked his horn and waved.

"Come on!" I told Dani. We ran and got in the car, me in front and Dani in back.

"How about a ride home?" asked Uncle Sergio. "With a stop for ice cream on the way?"

"Thanks, Uncle Sergio," we both said. Uncle Sergio is like an uncle to Dani, too.

"Is that a friend of yours?" Uncle Sergio pointed to the strange-looking girl who was staring at us.

Dani and I looked at each other and laughed. As if I, Javiera, would be friends with someone like that! "That's Julie," I told Uncle Sergio. "She's not anybody's friend."

"That's too bad," said Uncle Sergio. "Everybody needs a friend."

Nobody had ever wanted to be Julie's friend, and I didn't think that anyone ever would. Sometimes I had noticed how sad Julie looked, but there wasn't anything I could do about it. I didn't want to explain all that, so I just said, "Can we go now, please? I hear a chocolate cone calling my name!"

Uncle Sergio laughed and drove us to the ice cream shop. What a nice uncle!

About a week later, Uncle Sergio picked Dani and me up from school again. He was

coming to my house for dinner that night, so he was taking us to the bakery to get a cake. Before he started the car, he said, "I have something for you, Javiera. Look in that bag." I grabbed the bag off the dashboard, ripped it open, and pulled out a book.

"What is it?" asked Dani.

I read the title to her, "*Saint Francis Xavier*." To tell you the truth, I was a little disappointed. Uncle Sergio has given me some fantastic gifts before, and I was expecting something a little more...well, fantastic. But I said, "Thanks, Uncle Sergio," just the same.

"You're welcome," he said.

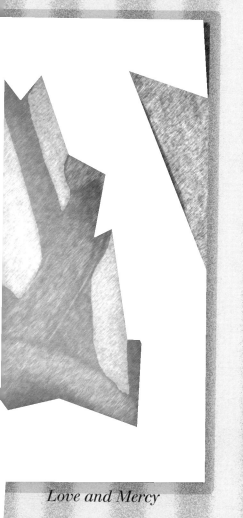

"Let me see," said Dani.

I passed her the book as Uncle Sergio turned the key. He looked in the mirror and told Dani, "Javiera is named after that fellow."

"I am?" That was news to me!

"Sure," said Uncle Sergio. "'Javiera' is the Spanish form of 'Xavier.'"

"Cool!" said Dani, handing the book back.

As I turned around, I noticed Julie sitting on the front steps, watching us. How long had she been there? She looked so sad—like someone who had never had someone nice like Uncle Sergio to give her a gift.

As we drove away, Uncle Sergio noticed Julie, too. "I feel so sorry for that lonely little girl."

"Me, too," I said quietly. But what could I, Javiera, do? So I pushed Julie out of my mind and paged through the book about the saint with my name.

Maybe I wasn't that excited about Uncle Sergio's gift at first, but the more I read, the more interested I got. That night, I stayed up late reading about Saint Francis Xavier's amazing life.

"He was from a noble family of Spain, but he lived in total poverty," I told Dani before school the next day. "On his missionary travels, he sometimes ate barely enough to stay alive!"

"But why?" asked Dani.

"For one thing, it brought him close to other poor people," I explained. "They felt like he understood them, and they listened when he talked to them about God."

"I don't think I could handle that," said Dani. "Not eating, I mean."

"Me neither," I said. "I hope Uncle Sergio takes us for ice cream again soon!"

And when we came out of school that afternoon, there he was! "How about some ice cream?" he asked as we got into the car.

"Thanks, Uncle Sergio!" we both yelled.

"And thanks, again," I added, "for the book. It's really good."

"He was quite a man, wasn't he?" said Uncle Sergio.

"Oh, yes!" I said. "He traveled all over." I turned to Dani. "And that was in the olden days when travel was really rough. It took forever to get anywhere."

"So why did he do it?" she asked.

"To teach everybody he could about Jesus," I said.

"They say that Saint Francis Xavier baptized thousands of people in India and Japan and everywhere in-between!" said Uncle Sergio.

"My book says that he was often exhausted," I said. "But he kept going."

"I don't think I could do that," said Dani.

"Me neither," I said.

"You could follow in his footsteps," said Uncle Sergio.

"You mean go to India?" I cried.

"I mean you could reach out to other people like Saint Francis did," said Uncle Sergio. "You don't have to travel the world to do that." He nodded his head toward the school building.

You guessed it! Julie was standing near the light pole, looking at us. When she saw that I saw her, she pretended to watch some kids getting on a bus.

Did Uncle Sergio mean that I should reach out to Julie? Hey, I wasn't Saint Javiera!

I turned back and said, "Anyway, thanks for the book. I think we'd better move so the kindergarten bus can pull up."

Uncle Sergio opened his mouth like he was going to say something more about Julie, but instead he just said, "Let's go get that ice cream! Some Rocky Road is calling for me!"

That night when I got into bed, I didn't pick my Saint Francis Xavier book off my bedside table. Maybe I won't read any more of it, I thought. I didn't want to be reminded of Uncle Sergio and Julie and all that. But then I started thinking about how I was named after Saint Francis and I just had to find out what else happened to him!

I wasn't surprised to read how much Saint Francis

Xavier wanted to reach out to the people of China. Even though he was very tired, he set off on another difficult journey! But he only made it as far as an island near China. Then he got sick and died. It was so sad.

When I finished the book, I closed it gently and sat there a long time just looking at the cover. Saint Francis Xavier had cared so much about reaching out to other people. Couldn't his namesake reach out even a teensy little bit?

Yes, you can, Javiera, I told myself.

Who knew how Julie would react if I tried to be friendly to her? And what would the other kids say? I didn't know, but I decided that I had to try.

I, Javiera.

Reprinted from My Friend: The Catholic Magazine for Kids, *Pauline Books & Media, 50 Saint Pauls Avenue, Boston, MA 02130.* www.myfriendmagazine.com

Discussion Starters for Grades K–3

Think of a time when you felt left out, like Julie in the story. Maybe it was on the playground. Maybe it was a time when you were really hoping that someone would ask you to be on a team, but that person didn't. How did you feel?

- How do you think others feel when you don't include them?
- How did Francis Xavier include others?
- What can we learn from the saints?
- Do you have a favorite saint? Who is it? What do you know about him/her?

Discussion Starters for Grades 4–8

In the story, "I, Javiera," how was Javiera influenced by knowledge of her patron saint?

- What do you know about your patron saint? (Have books of the saints handy so children can look up additional information.)
- How did your patron saint demonstrate his/her love for God and for others? Did he/she perform acts of mercy? Give some examples.
- Now let's think about our lives. Do we really live a life of faith? If so, how do we?
- How do we demonstrate our love for God? (Record the children's responses on a chalkboard or chart so everyone can see them.)
- How do we demonstrate our love for others? (Record their responses.)
- How do we demonstrate mercy? (Record their answers.)

Read these passages from the Bible (or retell the stories):

Luke 5:12–13 (Jesus heals the man with leprosy)

Luke 7:1–10 (The cure of the centurion's son)

Luke 7:11–15 (Jesus raises the widow's son)

Matthew 9:27–31 (Jesus heals two blind men)

- What are some signs of how Jesus felt about the people he helped? How can we grow in these same attitudes?
- Can you think of people in your community, maybe even at school, who are in need of some compassion or mercy? (Children shouldn't mention names.) Why do you think they are ignored or forgotten? Is that fair? Why or why not?
- How can YOU reach out to them in love and mercy?

We know from the Gospel story in Matthew (25:31–45) what Christ calls us to do. (Read Matthew, Chapter 25:31–45.)

String Art

Easy

During Lent, we strive to walk more closely in Christ's footsteps. We recommit to embracing our faith. One way we follow in Christ's footsteps is by reaching out to others in love and mercy. This craft project helps children to think of others. When completed, these projects will be given as gifts to others to remind them that somebody cares. As the children piece together their projects, they spend quiet moments praying for those who will receive their gifts of love.

Supplies needed:

foam sheet or poster board 7" x 11" (1 piece per child)

string of different colors, widths, textures

yarn of different colors, widths, textures

quick-drying, clear-drying craft glue

scissors

craft scissors with patterned edges

pencils

gel pens, markers, crayons, colored pencils

hole punch

Directions:

1. Have children trim poster board or foam sheet with craft scissors to form decorative patterned edges (to save time, you may want to pre-cut the poster board or foam sheets).

2. Draw a heart on poster board or foam sheet, using the template on page 36.

3. Glue different colors and types of yarn/string onto the heart. Start at the outer edge of the heart and work inward until the heart is completely filled in with yarn/string.

Younger artists will find thicker yarns and strings easier to work with. Older ones may want to work with a variety of yarn and string to form interesting patterns.

4. When glue is dry, write a short message like "Jesus cares and so do I" on the poster board or foam sheet.

5. Punch holes in top corners and attach a piece of yarn for hanging.

6. Have children give their artwork to someone who needs a little TLC.

Love-Is-Merciful Mobiles

Lent is a time of reflection. We examine our relationship with God and with others. One way we can grow closer to God is by showing others mercy and forgiveness. These mobiles can serve as simple reminders that love calls us to be merciful and kind.

Supplies needed:

foam sheet or poster board 10" x 10" (3 pieces per child)

pencils   markers

scissors   hole punch

craft scissors with patterned edges

kite string or yarn

coat hanger (1 per child)

Additional supplies for older children:

Bibles

Directions for younger children:

1. Each child needs to draw 3 hearts. The templates on page 36 could be used or the following "measurements" can be used. Cut large heart out of the poster board or foam sheet. Fold another sheet of poster board or foam sheet in half and cut the heart from 1 1/2 pieces. Fold the remaining half in half again and cut a heart from what remains. You should have 1/4 piece left over.

2. With markers write "Love" on small heart, "is" on medium heart, and "merciful" on large heart. Children can add decorations if they wish.

3. Cut out hearts using craft scissors with patterned edges (help cut out the smallest heart).

4. Punch holes in hearts and attach strings to form mobile. Hang the hearts from coat hanger.

5. Hang finished mobiles where they can be seen often to serve as simple reminders that we are called to be loving and merciful.

Directions for older children:

1. Use the templates provided on page 36 to trace 3 concentric hearts on the poster boards or foam sheets (foam sheets work best).

Notice that the smallest heart is the only one that forms a solid shape. (See photo.)

2. In order for the hearts to hang freely in the mobile, students will need to trim about a 1/4 inch border from each heart. (Use craft scissors with patterned edges for added interest.)

3. Punch holes in hearts and tie hearts together with string. (See photo.)

4. Search for Bible verses about love and mercy, then have children write verses on their heart mobiles.

5. Hang finished mobiles where they can be seen often as reminders that we are called to action through acts of mercy and love.

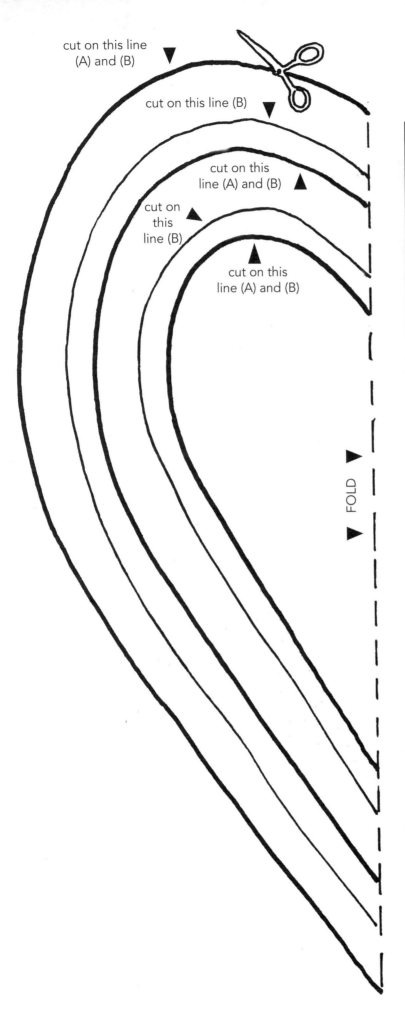

cut on this line
(A) and (B) ▼

cut on this line (B) ▼

cut on this
line (A) and (B) ▲

cut on
this
line (B) ▲

cut on this
line (A) and (B) ▲

► FOLD ►

Love-Is-Merciful Mobile
for Younger Children (A)

Love

is

merciful

Love-Is-Merciful Mobile
for Older Children (B)

Block Prints

This activity encourages children to think of others and to be compassionate to those in need. Donate these handmade, block-printed placemats and/or favors to local shelters, soup kitchens, nursing homes, or children's services. Once you've decided where to send your gifts, don't forget to call them and find out how many are needed. These block-printed messages of love are sure to brighten someone's day.

Supplies needed:

1/4"-thick foam sheets, cut into 4" x 4" squares

twine or thin jute, cord or cord-type string

craft glue   scissors

acrylic paints*   paint brushes

markers, crayons, pens

card stock (for favors)

construction paper measuring 11" x 17" (for placemats)

paint shirts or smocks

newspaper

Directions:

1. Have children spread newspaper over work surfaces and put on their paint shirts.

2. Glue 2 foam sheets together.

3. Draw simple line designs on foam sheets, 1 design per foam sheet.

4. Glue twine or thin jute along the line design on the foam sheets.

5. When glue dries, brush poster paint onto jute design on "printing block," then press "printing block" onto card stock or construction paper.

6. Repeat step 4 until desired design is achieved.

7. When dry, write messages with markers, crayons, or pens.

8. Fold card stock in half to form favors for place settings. (See illustration.)

Alternative:

Older children may want to try "block printing" written messages with their jute. Messages could include: Peace, God Cares, or God Bless You. Print letters backward on "printing blocks," because the print will be reversed. If writing more than one word, use one "block" per word.

* *Whenever working with paints, have children spread newspaper on work surfaces and wear paint shirts, smocks, or other protective clothing.*

Heart-Full-of-Love Envelope

Acts of kindness are acts of love. Help your children learn to be more considerate of others with this activity that is perfect for all ages because mercy knows no bounds.

Supplies needed:

2 pieces red construction paper (you only need 1 envelope per class or family)

double-sided tape

large greeting card envelope

Directions:

1. Seal the greeting card envelop as if mailing, then trim 1 inch off the top of the envelope to form a "pocket."

2. Cut 2 large hearts out of red construction paper. (Use largest template on page 36.)

3. Tape 1 of the hearts to the front of the "pocket" using double-sided tape. Then tape the other heart to the back of the "pocket."

4. Tape the sides and lower edges of hearts together to form your heart-shaped envelope.

5. Write: Heart-Full-of-Love on your heart-shaped envelope.

Now you will need to recruit the help of energetic children to compile a list of forty "Simple Acts of Kindness" that your class/family will perform during the coming days of Lent. These acts of kindness can be as simple as holding the door for someone, smiling at someone who looks lonely, or sharing a snack with someone who needs one. Your list should consist of forty suggestions because you'll need one for each day of Lent. Write each suggestion on a slip of paper and place it in your heart-shaped envelope.

Every day, a different child pulls a suggestion from the heart and then reads it aloud. Everyone should perform this "act of kindness" sometime during the day, although each will perform it at different times and under different circumstances.

The goal is to get everyone to think more about others and to act with compassion and love.

Since it's already the second week of Lent, all the slips won't be used by Easter, but that doesn't matter. Why stop at Easter? Jesus calls us to live a new life in him. With each new day come new opportunities to share God's mercy and love.

Secret Pals

Almsgiving–or compassion giving–is one of the ways we express our faith. This activity combines "fun" and "giving" and it helps to foster a sense of compassion. The "giving" is done in secret. The person who receives the gift doesn't know who sent it. They only know that it comes from someone who cares!

In the classroom:

Teachers will need to determine who will be a "secret pal" for whom. Teachers will also need to determine how long students will be "secret pals." The entire season of Lent might be a logical length of time, though a shorter period is fine, too. The advantage of having teachers compile the list of "secret pals" is that they can pair up students who wouldn't typically socialize. This exercise can help students learn more about each other, and, in the process, it can also foster new friendships.

Once the "secret pals" have been assigned, each "secret pal" tries to learn more about the other person, including his/her likes, interests, needs, prayer requests, etc. Then the "secret pals" get busy doing thoughtful things for their "pals." This might include being of help when assistance is needed, offering compliments, leaving a note or card on his/her desk that could say: "Special prayers for special YOU," or "I said a prayer for you today" (that way, the other person knows someone's praying for him/her), leaving inexpensive gifts such as a new pencil or bookmark on his/her desk, praying for him/her. The possibilities are limitless. What matters is to do things in the spirit of love and compassion. Eventually, students will be able to figure out who their "secret pal" is, and that's fine. If they don't figure this out by the end of the established time frame, then the "secret pals" can identify themselves.

In the home:

A family could "adopt" a family or neighbor in need, someone who is ill, or has had surgery, or anyone who needs a little TLC. Use the same process, only here your family works as a team to brighten someone's day. You can deliver to someone's front door cards of encouragement, prayer cards, artwork, fresh-cut flowers, etc., and leave a note that reads: From your Secret Pals.

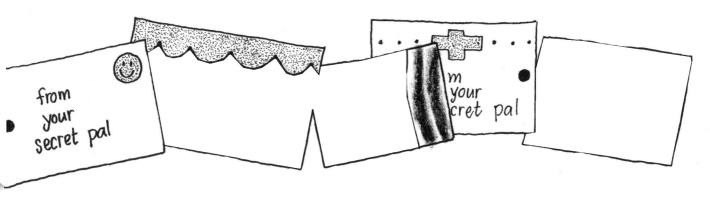

Encouraging Works of Mercy

To encourage children to share God's love with one another, begin with a class or family discussion about corporal and spiritual works of mercy. (Refer to the list.) Encourage children to suggest practical ways that they can perform these works of mercy in their daily lives, either at school, church, or home. Then follow up with the suggested activities.

Corporal Works of Mercy

Feeding the hungry
Giving drink to the thirsty
Sheltering the homeless
Clothing the naked
Visiting the sick
Visiting the imprisoned
Burying the dead

Spiritual Works of Mercy

Converting sinners
Instructing the ignorant
Advising the doubtful
Comforting the sorrowful
Bearing wrongs patiently
Forgiving injuries
Praying for the living and the dead

For younger children:

- Draw pictures that illustrate works of mercy and display them at home, throughout the school building, or even in the vestibule at the church.
- Play a game of charades, demonstrating various works of mercy.

For older children:

- Write a script that illustrates one or more of the works of mercy and then perform it in class or for other classes.
- Write a "news brief" or "announcement" to be read over the PA system at school or shared at the dinner table at home. These news briefs could include stories about young people who are making a difference in the world; a "Tip for the Day," which could suggest simple ways to reach out in love and compassion; or quotes from the Bible or the saints.
- Discuss how countries could show mercy. Include in your considerations the debt of Third World countries, relief aid, access to technology, etc.
- Design and copy a cartoon illustrating works of mercy to share with younger children. The younger children could color in the cartoons.
- Hold a letter-writing campaign to local, state, or national officials to voice the children's concern about social-justice issues.

"For the Son of man did not come to be served but to serve and to give his life as a ransom for many" (Mark 10:45).

Love and Mercy

Dear Parent(s),

During the Lenten season, we will be focusing on different aspects of Lent: its meaning, its symbols, its customs, and its traditions. Each week, your child will bring home Family Take-Home Pages, which are filled with activities that reinforce what we are discussing and learning in class. These Take-Home Pages are theme based and divided into three sections: Warm-Up Exercises, Getting Started, and Putting It into Practice. The theme for this week of Lent is Love and Mercy. May the activities suggested in these pages provide you with additional tools for nurturing your child's faith.

Warm-Up Exercises...

Gather the family around the Lenten candle. Have one member of the family light the candle and another read from Scripture. Then follow with a family discussion.

A reading from the letter of James 2:14–17

My friends, what good is it to say you have faith, when you don't do anything to show that you really do have faith? Can that kind of faith save you? If you know someone who doesn't have any clothes or food, you shouldn't just say, "I hope all goes well for you. I hope you will be warm and have plenty to eat." What good is it to say this, unless you do something to help? Faith that doesn't lead us to do good deeds is all alone and dead!

After sharing this passage with your family, lead them in a discussion in which everyone can participate. You may want to use the following questions:

What does St. James tell us about faith and good deeds?

How are we living our faith?

How are we helping others in need?

How can simple acts of love and mercy lead others to believe?

Getting Started...

Have another member of the family read this verse from the Gospel of Matthew (25:44–45).

Then the ones who pleased the Lord will ask, "When did we give you something to eat or drink? When did we welcome you as a stranger or give you clothes to wear or visit you while you were sick or in jail?"

The king will answer, "Whenever you did it for any of my people, no matter how unimportant they seemed, you did it for me."

Ask your children if they can think of ways that your family can help others in need. Jot down their ideas. Together, look over all the suggestions and then decide what your family could do to bring God's love and mercy to someone in need.

Here are a few ideas to get you started:

1. Start your spring-cleaning early with a special goal in mind.

Have everyone go through their closets and drawers and gather clothing they can pass on to someone at a shelter. These clothes should be in great shape. Place clothes in a gift bag along with a new pair of socks or underwear. You might need to do a bit of shopping, but the shopping trip can be a family affair. Let your children help with the selections. You might want to pick up some toiletries, too. In the gift bags for young children, you might want to add some fun items like stickers, crayons, and a coloring book. Make sure you include a note of encouragement. It can be as simple as "From someone who cares."

2. Find an elderly parishioner or neighbor who doesn't have family nearby or someone who doesn't get around easily. Think of things your family could do for him/her. Maybe you could provide transportation to and from church on Sunday mornings. Your children will learn from your example of thoughtful consideration. They'll also have the perfect opportunity to brighten someone's day through conversations while traveling to and from church. Your family might also discover other ways they can help this elderly person from those conversations in the car! Thoughtful gestures such as "spring-cleaning" their lawn or garden, sharing a batch of

fresh-baked cookies, or treating your elderly neighbor or parishioner to lunch are other ways your family can reach out in love and compassion.

Thoughtful gestures are acts of kindness. Acts of kindness are fruits of love. Add more thoughtful gestures to your day by smiling at someone, greeting those you pass on the sidewalk or in the hallway at school, holding the door for the person behind you, letting someone else have the last seat on the bus. Your family can easily think of dozens more.

Putting It into Practice...

Share this Bible verse with your family.

The Lord God has told us what is right and what he demands: "See that justice is done, let mercy be your first concern, and humbly obey your God" (Micah 6:8).

There's no way around it. In order for faith to be real, it must be coupled with good works and kind deeds. So have your family choose from your "list of suggestions" and turn those "suggestions" into actions, one by one.

Almsgiving During Lent

Making an extra-special effort to donate to the missions or to charities during the Lenten season is a tradition held by many families. For many children, receiving the annual "rice bowl" is a sure sign that Lent is here. Many parishes provide these familiar cardboard boxes to families at church or to children in religious education classes or parish schools.

Parents encourage their children to place weekly or even daily donations into these containers. For younger children, the act of placing money into the "rice bowl" (even when a parent gives them the money) reinforces the message that we are all called to love our neighbors, no matter how young we are or if those neighbors live next door or far away. When older children are encouraged to place money of their own into their "rice bowls," they learn that they also are called to make sacrifices so that others can have what they need to live in dignity: food, shelter, job, education.

It is equally important for children to see that their parents are also placing money into the "rice bowl." The money collected in these familiar cardboard boxes is donated to the Catholic Relief Fund at the end of the Lenten season.

Some families choose to support other groups or organizations. A designated jar, "kitty," or piggy bank collects the donations throughout the season. Then, at the end of Lent, the donations go to that particular organization.

You could take the money you've collected during Lent and purchase items on an organization's "wish list," and then donate them to that organization. These items might include crayons and coloring books for a crisis center, blankets for a pregnancy center, canned goods for a food bank, or toothbrushes and toothpaste for a homeless shelter.

Regardless of which charities a family chooses to support, gifts of love and compassion help brighten the lives of others and carry Christ's light into the world.

For additional ideas of charities and organizations you may want to support, check out the following websites:

Catholic Relief Services: www.catholicrelief.org

Habitat for Humanity: www.habitat.org

Special Olympics: www.specialolympics.org

Care Bags Foundation: www.carebags4kids.org

Mychal's Message: www.mychalsmessage.org

Bread for the World: www.bread.org

Volunteer Match: www.volunteermatch.org

Points of Light Foundation & Volunteer Center National Network: www.pointsoflight.org

Sisters of Life: www.sistersoflife.org

Reconciliation and Peace

Each week during the Lenten and Easter seasons, we will be focusing on a different theme. The theme for this week of Lent is Reconciliation and Peace.

A variety of activities is provided so you can choose those that best fit your children's needs. Some activities call for quiet reflection, and others involve group projects or discussions. Some require advance planning because you will need to gather supplies for craft projects. You may want to flip to the back of the book to the reproducible pages for possible additional materials.

Lent is a time when we examine how we are living our faith. It is important that children understand that peace comes through Reconciliation, and that Reconciliation calls for sorrow, for mending one's ways, and for healing through God's grace.

For those following a lectionary-based catechesis, this theme corresponds to the readings for the fourth Sunday of Lent.

Week-at-a-Glance

Supplies needed:

blindfold or sleep mask

wet wipes

hypo-allergenic hand lotion

soft music

Gather the children around the prayer table and light the Lenten candle (see page 11).

Say to the children: Sin hardens our hearts and darkens our world, but forgiveness brings healing and light. So we turn to God to ask for forgiveness; we turn to each other for forgiveness, too. The sacrament of Reconciliation offers us God's gift of healing. It also blesses us with the gift of grace. We, too, can bring the gift of healing into the world every time we choose to forgive.*

To help you center your thoughts on Jesus and on your need for forgiveness, close your eyes while I lead you in an examination of conscience. (See small booklet, pages 139–140. Please adjust according to age level.)

After a few moments of silent reflection, share the reading from Scripture.

A reading from Psalm 51:1

A Prayer for Forgiveness

You are kind, God!

Please have pity on me.

You are always merciful!

Please wipe away my sins.

Explain to the children: When we say or do things that hurt others, we sin and turn away from God, the Light of the world. Sin darkens our world. It keeps us from the Light. The blindfold that we will be using represents our sins.

Each of us will take a turn wearing the blindfold and being led to the prayer table where our hands will be wiped clean, the

––––––
* Children should return to their seats.

blindfold will be removed, and hand lotion will be given to us. The wet wipes symbolize the sacrament of Reconciliation which wipes away our sins; the lotion softens our skin as forgiveness softens our hearts.

The Bible tells us that if we want our sins to be forgiven, we must forgive each other. And that's what we'll be doing—forgiving each other.

In the classroom:

To help set a reflective tone for this experience, play soothing music as children are led to the prayer table. Explain that you will begin by blindfolding one child and leading him/her to the prayer table where his/her hands will be wiped clean, the blindfold removed, and lotion given. Then that child will blindfold another, lead him/her to the prayer table, remove his/her blindfold, wipe his/her hands, and give him/her lotion. This process will continue until everyone has had this experience. The last child can then lead the teacher.

In the home:

The family is seated around the table for the entire experience. A parent should blindfold one member of the family, wash his/her hands, then remove the blindfold and give him/her hand lotion. This routine is repeated until everyone has had a turn.

Closing Prayer for Younger Children

Forgive us, Jesus, as we forgive each other.

Thank you, Jesus. Amen.

Closing Prayer for Older Children

Forgive us, Jesus, as we forgive others.

Help us to be instruments of your peace. Amen.

The Candy Challenge

By Diana R. Jenkins
Illustrated by Steve Delmonte

"**I** 'm giving up candy to show Jesus that I love him, and I'm sorry that he suffered and...."

My little brother, Ellery, was running his mouth like he always does at supper. I'm lucky if I get to say, "Please pass the butter!"

"So, Amelia, what's your goal for Lent?" Dad quickly asked when Ellery took a breath.

"I'm making a promise to be kind to others," I said. "It will be a challenge, I know, but I want to do something...well... meaningful."

"Giving up candy is a challenge, too," said Ellery.

"It certainly is," said Mom. "Isn't it, Amelia?"

"Yeah, sure," I said, even though I was thinking that Ellery's goal didn't compare to mine.

For days, Ellery kept telling people about giving up candy. "I made a promise to God," he said over and over. "And I'm going to keep it." One afternoon, he even told our bus driver!

As we walked up the driveway, I said, "Sheesh, Ellery, shut up about the candy already. You sound stupid."

At supper, I told Mom and Dad how I helped my teacher carry some boxes and shared my lunch with a kid who'd forgotten his. "It sounds like

you're really serious about being kind," said Mom.

"I am," I said. Before I could say more, Ellery took over the conversation, bragging about his big no-candy sacrifice.

O ne night, I came into the living room for a book. Ellery jumped up off the couch when he saw me and stuck one hand behind his back. "What are you doing?" I asked.

"N-n-nothing."

But I smelled...chocolate! I grabbed his arm and pried open his hand. "You're eating candy?"

"Just a little piece," he muttered.

"But you made a promise to give up candy. A promise to

God," I reminded him. "This is terrible! I'm telling!"

But when I marched to the kitchen and told Mom and Dad what Ellery had done, they just talked to him about trying again.

"But he broke a promise! A promise to God," I pointed out.

"God will understand," said Mom. "He knows this is hard for Ellery, and he just wants him to keep trying."

On Saturday, I was in the kitchen when Ellery walked in from the porch. There was chocolate all around his mouth!

"What's that brown stuff on your face?" I asked.

He wiped his hand across his lips. "I...uh...gravy!"

"From last night's supper? I don't think so," I said. "You were eating candy again! What kind of person are you?"

"A person who likes candy?" he peeped.

"NO!" I yelled. "A bad person. A very bad person!"

"What's going on?" Dad was standing in the doorway.

I told him about Ellery sneaking candy. "I knew he would do it again," I said.

"That's enough, Amelia," said Dad. "I'll talk to Ellery about this." But all he did was tell Ellery to try again!

On Sunday, I stood by the coat rack and helped people with their coats before and after Mass. It made me feel so good to do something nice that I decided to keep the job from now on.

As we went to the car, I told Mom and Dad my plan. "Great!" said Dad. "That's the idea of Lent, I think. To help us make positive changes that last all our lives."

When my parents stopped to talk to someone, Ellery tugged on my sleeve. "Did Dad

mean that I have to give up candy forever?"

"Of course not, you dope!" I said. "Anyway, you can't even give up candy for a few measly weeks."

"Well, it's hard," he whined.

"It's not nearly as hard as what I'm doing," I said. "Being kind to other people is a real challenge, believe me!"

The next week, I tutored a first-grader, did extra chores, walked our neighbor's dog, and...well, you get the idea. I took my Lenten goal seriously, unlike some people!

Twice I smelled chocolate on Ellery's breath. I jumped all over him about it, but it didn't do any good. On Thursday night, I caught him chocolate-handed in the laundry room.

"What's the matter with you?" I shouted, snatching away his half-eaten candy bar.

"You made a commitment! A promise! Doesn't that mean anything to you?"

"Yes!" he said. "And I'm trying!"

"It's a good thing you didn't pick anything really tough to do for Lent," I said. "There's no way you could handle the kind of thing I'm doing. What a loser!"

Ellery's face turned red. "I can't wait for Lent to be over!"

I snorted. "Sure! Then you can eat all the candy you want."

"That's not what I mean, Amelia," he said. "I want Lent to be over so you'll stop being mean to me!" Then he burst into tears and ran off.

"I'm not mean, you big, stupid...." My voice trailed away as I realized how I sounded. I *was* being mean. Which didn't fit at all with my goal for Lent, did it?

So I slipped up once, I told myself. But I knew that I'd been unkind to Ellery more than once. A lot of times, in fact.

I wished that I could travel back in time, start Lent over, and include my brother in my kindness plan. But I'd already messed everything up, and it was too late to make things right. Wasn't it?

Maybe not, I realized. Maybe I could try again. Like Mom and Dad told Ellery to do.

I found my brother lying facedown on his bed. "Go away," he mumbled into his pillow.

"Listen," I said. "You know how hard it's been for you to give up candy? Well, I guess I'm having trouble with my promise to be kind, too. I'm really sorry."

Ellery sat up and looked at me. "You are?"

"Yeah," I said. "How about if I help you with the candy thing?"

"How?" he asked.

"We can do something fun when you're tempted," I said. "Or I can fix you a healthy snack. Or something. Anyway, I'll think of a kind way to help you instead of yelling."

"Promise?" he said.

"Promise," I said.

So my brother and I have both been working hard on our goals for Lent. Sometimes I lose my patience with Ellery and forget my promise to be kind. That's when I pray for God's help and try again. It's been a real challenge, let me tell you, but I think God understands that I'm doing something hard. He just wants me to keep trying. That's what...I tell...he-e-ey....

You'll have to excuse me now. I smell chocolate!

The Lent–Easter Book

Reprinted from My Friend: The Catholic Magazine for Kids, *Pauline Books & Media, 50 Saint Pauls Avenue, Boston, MA 02130.* www.myfriendmagazine.com

Discussion Starters for Grades K–3

- What did you promise to do during Lent?
- What did you promise to give up or do extra for Lent?
- Why did you choose those things?
- Is it as hard for you to keep your promise as it was for Ellery and Amelia? Why?

- Do you think God knows how hard it is for you to do what you're doing? Why?
- What can you do if you happen to break your promise? Do you think God will understand? Why or why not?

Discussion Starters for Grades 4–8

Sometimes what we SAY and what we DO are two different things. Why do you think that is?

Think about a time you caught yourself telling your brother or sister or friend not to do something, but then you turned around and did that very same thing yourself. Maybe you told your younger brother or sister to stop tattling and you end up complaining to your parent(s) about him or her. That's tattling, too. Or maybe you tell your best friend not to gossip, but the next time you hear a wild story, you turn around and tell your friend about what you heard at school.

Read to the children from the Gospel of Luke (7:36–50). Talk about how Simon was acting like Amelia.

- What do you think the "sinful woman" felt like?
- Do you think it was courageous of her to go into the room and express her love to Jesus?
- How was the "sinful woman" like Ellery?
- Which person do you relate to more in this Gospel narrative? Simon the Pharisee or the woman who washed Jesus' feet with her tears?
- Are there times that you feel like Simon and other times that you feel like the woman?

- What made the woman so dear to Jesus is that she took him completely at his word.

Jesus said, "Come to me and I will refresh you, forgive you, heal you." Even the apostles didn't have the courage to show Jesus their weakness. They are often described in the Gospels as trying to get the first place. But this woman understood that Jesus was there for her and would not treat her as Simon did.

- Do you take Jesus at his word?
- Do you trust in his forgiveness and help to become more like him?

Give the children time to write a letter to the woman who loved Jesus, asking her to help them love Jesus and trust him as she did.

Reflection

When she beheld you hanging on the cross,
Your Virgin Mother lamented bitterly and cried to you:
What is this new and strange wonder, my Son?
How has the lawless people nailed you to the cross,
Life of all, my sweetest Light?

Orthodox Liturgy

A Peace Offering

This gift-wrapped box helps children to see that our words, actions, thoughts, and prayers can be instruments of peace.

Younger children may need help with this project. Older children could buddy-up to help them. This activity may extend over two days.

Teacher/Parent preparation:

1. Cut or tear tissue paper and gift wrap into 6 by 6-inch pieces ahead of time. Children will need three or four different 6 by 6-inch pieces of wrapping paper for their boxes.

2. Before decorating boxes, each child should write an apology to someone they have offended. Keep these in desks until later. Apologies will be placed inside the boxes.

Supplies needed:

small box with lid (1 for each child)

all-occasion gift wrap

different colors of gift-wrap tissue paper

ribbon

decoupage

foam brushes

pencils or pens

acrylic or poster paints*

notebook paper or stationery

paint shirts or smocks

newspaper

Directions:

1. Have children spread newspaper over work surfaces and put on their paint shirts.

_____

* *Whenever working with paints, have children spread newspaper on work surfaces and wear paint shirts, smocks, or other protective clothing.*

2. Have children tear their gift wrap or tissue paper into nickel-size tiny pieces.

3. Remove the lid from the box; set bottom aside.

4. Using a foam brush, coat the top of the lid with a thin layer of decoupage and apply tiny pieces of paper.

5. Cover the sides of the lid using the same process. Set aside to dry.

6. Repeat the same process with the bottom of the box.

7. Once the lid and box are dry, brush on another thin layer of decoupage.

8. When lid and box are completely dry, place apologies inside and tie ribbon around the box. It should look like a "present."

9. Invite children to give their "presents" or "peace offerings" to the ones they've offended and to make amends.

Weaving Words of Peace

An art lesson + a vocabulary lesson = a lesson in peace. Help your children learn words of peace as they complete this project.

Supplies needed:

11" x 17" craft foam sheets or construction paper, various colors (1 for each child)

scissors   markers

glue   yarn

ribbon, raffia, fabric strips (enough for decorating the foam sheets/construction paper)

Before starting this project, discuss the qualities and actions that promote peace, such as kindness, compassion, love, respect, tolerance, acceptance, forgiveness, mercy, etc. Also discuss familiar Bible verses that speak of peace such as:

"Only God gives inward peace, and I depend on him" (Psalm 62:5).

"Do good instead of evil and try to live at peace" (Psalm 34:14).

"…and do your best to live at peace with everyone" (Romans 12:18).

"God blesses those people who make peace. They will be called his children!" (Matthew 5:9)

Directions:

1. Have children form the "base" for the weaving by cutting foam sheet or construction paper widthwise into strips, stopping 1 inch from the top. (See diagram, top right.)

2. Cut a variety of materials into strips that measure the length of the "base." Ribbon, yarn, raffia, fabric scraps add to the interest.

3. Weave strips through the foam sheet or paper "base."

4. Secure the ends of their strips with glue.

5. Cut 1 strip that measures 1 by 17 inches and glue to the bottom of the weaving.

6. Write words or statements of peace* across weaving on the foam strips or paper that form the "base." (See photo.)

7. Write "Weaving Words of Peace" on the border of artwork.

"Base" for Weaving

leave 1" of space on this side

* Remind children that just as the words they printed became part of their artwork, so, too, the words that we think and say become a part of who we are. They can affect our thoughts and actions. Let's choose words of peace to help heal our hearts, homes, schools, neighborhoods, and world!

The Telephone Game

Easy

This fun game reminds children that our words really do matter.

Directions:

1. Gather children into a large circle and explain how to play the game of "telephone."

2. You whisper a message to the person on your left; they whisper the same message to the person on their left, and so on. Eventually the message comes back to you and you tell the group what you heard. You also ask the person next to you to repeat the message you first told him/her. The two messages will probably be quite different.

3. Repeat the process several times with different messages. Encourage the children to listen carefully and to ask questions if they don't understand what they heard.

Children can learn valuable lessons from this game. Perhaps the most obvious is that our words really do matter. Second, we should listen more carefully. Third, messages can get distorted when passed from person to person.

Tell the children: Rumors and gossip grow and change when repeated, just like the messages in our game of telephone. Rumors and gossip cause division rather than peace; they hurt rather than heal.

Discuss ways children can put a stop to unkind words. Suggest statements such as, "Time out! Let's talk about something else."

Or "Come on! We don't want to spread rumors. We wouldn't like it if someone spread rumors about us." Children should have no trouble coming up with their own statements.

Now give them the opportunity to nip in the bud the "rumors" YOU try to share with them.

Here are a few to get you started:

1. You're never going to believe what I just heard about Pete!

2. Merrie said that So-'n-So said such-'n-such about You-Know-Who…

3. Rumor has it that…

4. Did you know that…

Have children commit to NOT to participating in gossip or rumors. As a sign of their commitment, have them sign the "Telephone" contract (see page 53).

Alternative for older children:

Hold a media watch. Have children view a program they usually watch, but they should take note of the different ways gossip and rumors affect the characters in the show. After discussing words that are destructive and painful, and words that heal and show compassion, ask the children to write a different ending to the show that would have resulted if only one person had chosen to say healing words.

"Telephone" Contract

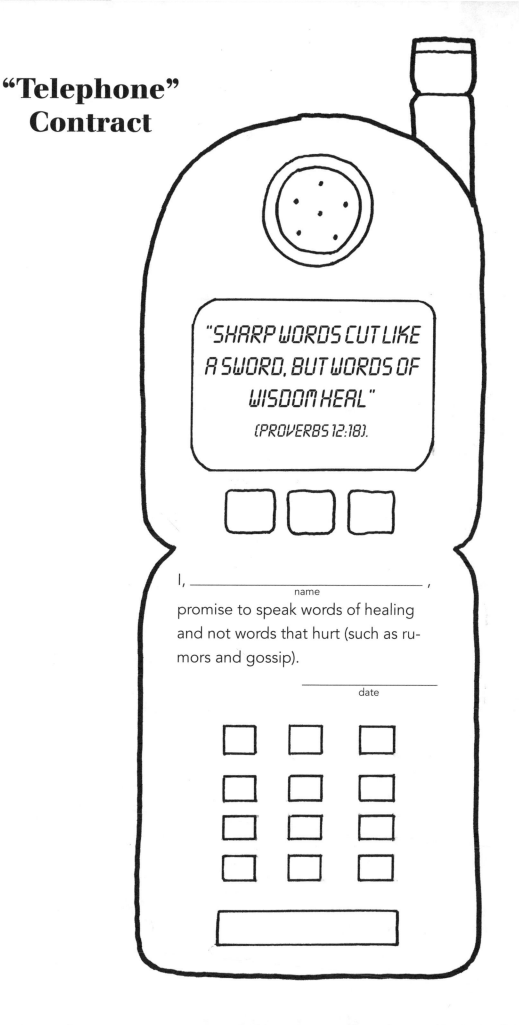

"SHARP WORDS CUT LIKE A SWORD, BUT WORDS OF WISDOM HEAL" (PROVERBS 12:18).

I, _____ ,
name

promise to speak words of healing and not words that hurt (such as rumors and gossip).

_____
date

Recipe for Peace

Easy

Good recipes contain just the right combinations and amounts of special ingredients. Help your budding chefs come up with a winning recipe for peace. Then serve up a big helping to everyone you meet!

Baker's Tip: Prayer is an essential ingredient in the Recipe for Peace.

Supplies needed:

1 sheet of poster board

markers   pens or pencils

recipe cards or index cards (1 per child)

string for hanging poster

Directions:

1. Explain to the children that they're going to concoct a recipe for peace. Brainstorm with them all the possible ingredients they might want to include (e.g., love, humor, patience).

2. Write down all their suggestions. When they have exhausted their possibilities, review their suggestions and have them select several for their recipe.

3. Next, discuss with them the fact that recipes call for a certain amount of each ingredient, so they will need to determine amounts. They could use standard measurements (cups, tablespoons, etc.), or general measurements (a handful of this, or a dab or sprinkle of that…).

4. Have the children suggest the order and amounts of ingredients while you write them on the poster board "recipe card."

5. Remember to include: Name of Recipe, From (your class/family), Number of Servings (plenty for everyone), Serving Size (enough for peace and joy).

6. Once the huge "recipe card" is finished, punch 2 holes on each end of the top of the card and attach a string for hanging. Hang it in a place of honor to remind everyone how each person can work for peace. Then pass out regular-size recipe cards and have the children write their recipes on them. Allow the children time to decorate their recipe cards. These cards can serve as reminders and can be hung on a refrigerator or used as a bookmark.

"…do your best to live at peace with everyone" (Romans 12:18).

Reconciliation and Peace

Dear Parent(s),

During the Lenten season, we will be focusing on different aspects of Lent: its meaning, its symbols, its customs, and its traditions. Each week, your child will bring home Family Take-Home Pages, which are filled with activities that reinforce what we are discussing and learning in class. These Take-Home Pages are theme based and divided into three sections: Warm-Up Exercises, Getting Started, and Putting It into Practice. The theme for this week of Lent is Reconciliation with its gift of peace. May the activities suggested in these pages provide you with additional tools for nurturing your child's faith.

Warm-Up Exercises...

Gather the family around the Lenten candle. Have one member of the family light the candle and another read from Scripture. Then follow with a family discussion.

A reading from the letter to the Romans 12:17–18

Brothers and sisters: Don't mistreat someone who has mistreated you. But try to earn the respect of others, and do your best to live at peace with everyone.

Discuss the following questions with your family:

When I get upset with someone, do I yell or throw a tantrum? Or do I shut up and give the "silent treatment"? Or do I speak honestly about the way I feel?

Explain to the children: Neither a tantrum nor the "silent treatment" fosters an atmosphere of peace. But by speaking honestly and openly about our feelings, we can foster an atmosphere of understanding and respect. When we understand and respect each other, peaceful solutions are possible.

Here are a few exercises to help you work for peace:

Practice using statements such as, "I feel … when you …" to help each member understand the other's point of view. Have each member of the family think of a few examples they can share with each other. Parent(s) should start with an example or two, then encourage children to do the same. Some suggested statements are provided to get you started:

"I feel so frustrated when you know you're going to be late but don't bother to call to let me know."

"I feel scared when I hear you arguing and fighting. I'm afraid someone will get hurt."

"I feel helpless when you don't come to me with your problems. I want to help, but I can't if you won't share your problems with me."

Practice speaking words of peace such as:

I love you.

I forgive you.

I'm sorry.

Let's start over.

I care.

I'd like to help.

Do you want to talk about it?

God bless you.

Please and thank you.

Have your family think of other words to add to your list. Then use these words of healing on a daily basis.

Getting Started...

The Bible teaches us a lot about forgiveness. You can find clues in these readings from Scripture. Have someone read them aloud.

"...Forgive our sins, as we forgive everyone who has done wrong to us..." (Luke 11:4).

"So if you are about to place your gift on the altar and remember that someone is angry with you, leave your gift there in front of the altar. Make peace with that person, then come back and offer your gift to God" (Matthew 5:23–24).

Your family can suggest additional verses, too.

Now encourage the members of your family to think of someone they need to forgive. Encourage them to also think of someone from whom they need forgiveness. Remind them that reconciliation brings about healing and healing brings about peace. Help your family not to cling to hurt and to let go of grudges. The time for forgiveness is now.

As a symbolic gesture of forgiveness, break a loaf of bread (a biscuit, dinner roll or pita loaf will do) and share it with the one you need to forgive. Allow each member of the family to do the same. Accompany that symbolic gesture with a sincere apology or a hug.

Putting It into Practice...

Share this reading from the Gospel of Matthew (5:43–48).

You have heard people say, "Love your neighbors and hate your enemies." But I tell you to love your enemies and pray for anyone who mistreats you. Then you will be acting like your Father in heaven. He makes the sun rise on both good and bad people. And he sends rain for the ones who do right and for the ones who do wrong. If you love only those people who love you, will God reward you for that? Even tax collectors love their friends. If you greet only your friends, what's so great about that? Don't even unbelievers do that? But you must always act like your Father in heaven.

Sometimes we struggle to forgive others who have caused us great pain. Sometimes forgiveness takes tremendous effort and the prayerful support of others. Help family members release pent-up pain and hurt with this gesture of "letting go."

Directions:

Go to a nearby river or creek with your family. Take along a bag of bread crumbs. Stand by the flowing water and ask God to help your family let go of their hurts. Explain to your family that the bread crumbs represent the hurts and pains they hold in their hearts. Then let everyone take a handful of bread crumbs and toss them into the river. Watch the current carry the hurts away. Then as a family, thank God for his blessing of forgiveness, and ask him to help your family begin to heal today.

— *56* —

Traditions create memories. Memories enrich our lives. Traditions also help us pass on valuable lessons to our children and to our children's children.

During Lent, we are called to conversion. One of the first steps we can take toward that conversion is to receive the sacrament of Reconciliation, the sacrament that blesses us with the healing grace of God's mercy. It is through God's gifts of mercy and forgiveness we are able to start anew.

While the sacrament of Reconciliation is only required for grievous sins, and Catholics should go to confession at least once a year, many families still consider it an essential part of their Lenten preparation for the coming celebration of Easter joy.

During Lent, many parishes offer a communal penance service in which people prepare together for confession and give thanks together for the forgiveness received. After reading from Scripture, everyone is led through a common examination of conscience and expression of sorrow. Individual confession and absolution follow. If you don't already participate in the communal penance service as a family, you might want to consider doing so. Who knows? It may become one of your family's most meaningful Lenten traditions.

In preparing to receive the sacrament of Reconciliation, whether communal or private, we take time to reflect on our thoughts, our words, our actions, and our failures to take action. Have our thoughts, words, and actions brought us closer to God or have they hardened our hearts to his love? With self-examination, we realize the need for sorrow and

change, so we can once again walk closer with Jesus. (You may want to make use of the booklet for the sacrament of Reconciliation on pages 138–140.) God blesses with his wonderful gifts of mercy and peace all of those who confess their sins with contrite hearts. As we pray the Our Father, we remember that forgiveness isn't limited to God and ourselves. If we want forgiveness, then we, too, are to forgive those who have offended us.

So start with family members, and let the healing begin.

"…and forgive us our trespasses as we forgive those who trespass against us…"

Baptism

Each week during the Lenten and Easter seasons, we will be focusing on a different theme. The theme for this week of Lent is Baptism.

A variety of activities is provided so you can choose those that best fit your children's needs. Some activities call for quiet reflection, and others involve group projects or discussions. Some require advance planning because you will need to gather supplies for craft projects.

In the early Church, people were baptized at Easter. The period of preparation for Baptism developed into the season of Lent. Today, people who wish to enter the Catholic Church are baptized at the Easter Vigil. However, Lent is a preparation for us all to recommit ourselves to our baptismal promises, so children should understand those promises. It is also important that they understand that our lives should reflect our baptismal promises and the Catholic faith.

For those following a lectionary-based catechesis, this theme corresponds to the readings for the third Sunday of Lent.

Week-at-a-Glance

Supplies needed:

photo of each participant

tape or glue · paper towels

bowl of water · poster board

puzzle pieces · soft music

Teacher/Parent Preparation:

You will need to make two identical "puzzles" out of poster board; they can be in the shape of a large heart or a cross. One "puzzle" will be cut into pieces; the other will serve as the "base" onto which the puzzle pieces will be taped or glued. You will need as many puzzle pieces as you have children plus one for yourself and any other adults participating in the prayer experience. On the "base," you will need to draw the outline of the puzzle pieces so the children will be able to see where to place their piece of the puzzle. On each puzzle piece, you will need to glue a photo of one of the children.

Gather the children around the prayer table. Light the Lenten candle (see page 11).

Say to the children: Baptism is the sacrament that welcomes us into the family of the Church. During the season of Lent, we prepare to renew our baptismal promises on Easter. We affirm our resolve to turn away from sin and everything that leads us to sin. We express our belief in God the Father, God the Son, and God the Holy Spirit. We renew our belief in the holy Catholic Church, the communion of saints, the forgiveness of sins, the resurrection of the body, and life everlasting.

Now let us listen carefully to these words from Scripture.

A reading from the
Acts of the Apostles 22:16

What are you waiting for? Get up! Be baptized, and wash away your sins by praying to the Lord.

When we were first welcomed into the Church, the priest traced the Sign of the Cross on our forehead and then poured the waters of Baptism over us. At this time, I invite each of you to come forward, dip your right hand into the bowl of holy water, then bless yourself with the sign of your faith. The Sign of the Cross is a sign of belonging. It is also a sign of your commitment to Christ.

After you bless yourself with the holy water, you will receive a puzzle piece that you will add to our puzzle. As a puzzle needs each piece to make it whole, so, too, does the Church. We, as members of the Body of Christ, form the Church. Just as every piece of the puzzle is important, so, too, every member of the Church is important. We each have a special part to play.

Play soft, inspirational music while children come forward to bless themselves and receive their piece of the puzzle. After blessing themselves, children can glue or tape their puzzle piece onto the "puzzle." Once the puzzle is completed, end with the short prayer.*

Closing Prayer for Younger Children

Dear Jesus, thank you for the gift
of Baptism.
Help me to live my Catholic faith.

Closing Prayer for Older Children

Dear God, thank you for the gift
of Baptism.
Help me to grow stronger in my
Catholic faith.

---

* *These simple prayers should be repeated daily throughout the week as a reminder that we, as followers of Jesus and as members of the Catholic Church, are called to live what we believe.*

"Dare You"

By Clare Mishica and illustrated by Virginia Esquinaldo

I stared at the bright pink invitation and blinked my eyes. Tricia Spellor had invited me, Cory Wells, to her thirteenth birthday party sleepover. For me, an invitation to meet the President and spend a night at the White House would not seem a greater honor. Tricia Spellor was the most popular girl in the seventh grade.

"Can you come?" she asked me after school.

"You bet," I grinned, and she gave me a little wave as she walked away. Her shiny black hair fell like a curtain half way down her back, and she had a cool purse with beaded fringe slung over her shoulder. Everything about Tricia Spellor seemed absolutely perfect.

On Friday night, I couldn't figure out what to wear. I decided on a pair of jeans with frayed edges because Tricia wore some almost like them. I also decided to pull my hair back into a tight braid. At least that way no one would notice my curly frizz. My hair always looks like I've just gotten off a roller coaster.

When I got to Tricia's house, the first thing we did was tie-dye socks. Of course, Tricia's turned out with little yellow and orange starbursts all over them, and mine looked like I'd dropped them into a mud puddle. Then we had pizza. Thankfully, I made it through without choking and squirting soda out of my nose like Melissa Evers did. Next, we started playing "Truth or Dare." Basically, you have to answer a question or do a dare.

I laughed until my stomach hurt. Megan had kissed a goldfish, and Melissa had danced with a pair of stinky tennis shoes that belong to Tricia's brother. Tricia had admitted her most embarrassing moment happened when she accidentally walked into the boy's bathroom at the library. No one had been inside, but our science teacher, Mr. Mannin, had seen her walk out. Finally, it was my turn.

"Hey, Cory, truth or dare," said Melissa.

I didn't hesitate too long before I said, "Dare." I wasn't about to tell ten giggling girls any deep dark secrets about myself. Besides, I'm a pretty good sport.

Melissa whispered something to a girl named Anna who fell backward screeching with laughter. I decided that probably wasn't a good sign. Then Melissa said, "You have to visit the batboy and tell him good-bye."

"It's a little late at night," I said, swallowing hard. The

batboy was really Daniel Betterby, a boy in the ninth grade. He was way into bats, and everyone thought he was weird. In a week, he was moving away.

"Not now!" said Melissa, laughing. "Tomorrow afternoon."

"At least the bats will be sleeping then," I cracked. Everyone laughed, but my stomach felt all tight and twisted. I'd have rather slept all night with the smelly sneakers for a pillow.

The next morning, the girls reminded me that they expected a full story about my visit to the batboy. I had hoped they'd forgotten, but that hadn't happened.

"Remember to report me as missing if I don't show up at the bowling alley tonight," I joked, and they giggled.

Later, after I dropped my stuff off at home, I walked down the road toward Daniel's house. He only lived a block away. I figured that I'd pretend I was being neighborly and stopping by to wish him well. I strolled by Daniel's house twice before I got up the nerve to open the gate and walk down the path toward his house.

"Hey," called someone from the old barn near the back. "Who are you looking for?" It was Daniel.

I started talking while I was still four feet away, trying to get all the words out fast. "I heard you were moving, and I wanted to say good-bye. I hope you have a great trip."

Daniel stared at me, and I noticed he had friendly brown eyes. "How much did they pay you, Squirt?" he joked. "Do you need proof that you visited the batboy and survived?"

"No," I said, swallowing hard. At that moment, I felt pretty ashamed of myself, even though Daniel didn't seem to care a whole lot.

"I'm sorry for bothering you," I mumbled.

"It's okay," he said, as my face turned four shades of red. "My bat hobby doesn't win me a lot of fans."

"Then why do you do it?" I blurted out.

Daniel looked at me in a funny way. I figured my big mouth had gotten me into trouble again when he asked, "Do you really want to know?"

I nodded, and Daniel said, "Come on."

I followed him around to the back of the barn while he started telling me about bats.

"Bats are amazing creatures," he said. "One little brown bat can eat 600 mosquitoes in an hour. They don't nest in people's hair—that's a goofy myth. A bat knows where it's flying because it bounces sounds off objects. A bat can even hear a bug's footsteps."

"No way," I said, surprised, and Daniel laughed.

"Yes way," he said, "and bats help pollinate crops, too, like bananas, figs, and peaches."

"I guess I never thought much about bats," I said.

"I plan to be a wildlife biologist," Daniel told me. "I love studying animals. What do you like to do?"

"I'm not sure," I said, thinking. By that time, I'd pretty much forgotten that I was talking to the batboy. "I'm not very good at art," I answered, remembering my mud socks. "I do like writing."

"Are you on the school newspaper staff?"

"Umm, no," I said. I hadn't joined because my friends hadn't, but now that seemed like a dumb reason.

"See those big wooden boxes?" Daniel asked, pointing up to the back of the barn.

"Yeah."

"They're bat houses," he explained. "Little brown bats can live for over 32 years, but they need safe places to stay. A colony is living there now, and I'm afraid someone is going to knock them down after I leave."

"Maybe I could write a story about bats for the school newspaper," I said. "It might help."

"I'd appreciate that," said Daniel. "The bats need some good press."

"I'll send you a copy," I offered, "if you want."

"Sure," Daniel agreed. "I'll give you my new address." We walked inside the barn where Daniel had a notebook and pencil.

"Now you have great proof that you visited the batboy," he joked as he handed me the paper, "and survived."

"I am really glad I came," I told Daniel.

"Then send me that article. I have to go now. I do have some friends, and we're going to play basketball."

"Oh, sure," I mumbled, tucking the paper inside my pocket. Then I walked down the path and out the gate, thinking about my visit with Daniel. It was like someone had pulled up all the shades in a dark room, and my eyes were trying to adjust to the bright light. I actually felt kind of jealous. Daniel knew himself so well—what he wanted, and who he was.

"I dare you," I finally whispered to myself. "I dare you to be Cory Wells and not Tricia Spellor or Melissa Evers or anyone else." It was a dare I planned on taking.

Reprinted from My Friend: The Catholic Magazine for Kids, *Pauline Books & Media, 50 Saint Pauls Avenue, Boston, MA 02130.* www.myfriendmagazine.com

Discussion Starters for Grades K–3

- Do you have any unusual hobbies like Daniel? What are they?

- Have you ever been misunderstood or even teased about your hobbies? If so, how did that make you feel? What could you tell others about your hobbies that would help them understand that your hobbies are actually pretty neat?

- What does Cory learn from playing "Truth or Dare" with her friends? How is this an important way to understand our Baptism?

Discussion Starters for Grades 4–8

- How did Cory feel about being invited to Tricia's party? What is it like to feel like you belong?

- Do you know someone like "batboy"? Someone who has unusual hobbies or interests? How do you think the "batboy" felt, being on the outside of the group of kids his age, not really belonging to their group?

- Why do you think we want so much to belong?

- What did Cory learn from her "dare"?

- How did Cory's "dare" turn into something positive? Do you think it is important to really be who you are in order to truly belong to a group?

Read the following passage from the Gospel of John (15:1, 4–6, 7):

"I am the true vine, and my Father is the gardener…. Remain in me, and I will remain in you. No branch can bear fruit by itself; it must remain in the vine. Neither can you bear fruit unless you remain in me. I am the vine; you are the branches. If a man remains in me and I in him, he will bear much fruit; apart from me you can do nothing. If anyone does not remain in me, he is like a branch that is thrown away and withers; such branches are picked up, thrown into the fire and burned. If you remain in me and my words remain in you, ask whatever you wish, and it will be given you."

What does the image of the vineyard tell us about belonging to Jesus? We become part of the vine at our Baptism. In the waters of Baptism, we die and rise with Jesus and belong to him forever. When we are baptized we become the branches on the vine. As long as we stay connected to the vine we will be filled with life and fruit.

The "batboy" wasn't interested in belonging to a special group of friends; he was more interested in pursuing his hobby. Cory learned from the "batboy" that there was more to life than being in with the popular group of girls.

- Where do you want to "belong"? Are you true to the gifts God gave you?

- With your Baptism, do you belong to Jesus? Do you feel like you belong to Jesus? What is one thing you could do to grow closer to Jesus?

- Do you worship with your parish to express your belonging? What can you do to strengthen your belonging in the Church?

Holy Water Font

During the season of Lent, we reflect on Christ's journey to the cross. We also reflect on our baptismal promises. Every time we bless ourselves with holy water and the Sign of the Cross, we acknowledge our Baptism and our faith.

Supplies needed:

legal size copy paper (1 piece per holy water font)

about 11 clothespins (with metal spring removed) per holy water font

Crystal Lite™ plastic jar (about the size of an orange juice can; 1 per holy water font)

scissors

markers or paint*

paint shirts or smocks

glue

newspaper

Teacher/Parent Preparation:

Before working with children, an adult will need to cut the top inch off the empty Crystal Lite™ container.

Directions:

1. Have children spread newspaper over work surfaces and put on their paint shirts.

2. Have children cut a piece of copy paper tall enough to fit the height of the can and long enough to go around the outside of the can plus 1 inch.

3. If desired, color or paint clothespin halves.

4. Glue clothespin pieces onto copy paper, flat side down, one up and one down. (Be sure that the clothespins are flush against the bottom edge of the paper.) Leave the last inch of paper without clothespins, so the paper can overlap when placed around the can.

5. Glue the clothespin-covered-copy paper around the can, then let dry.

6. Children can get holy water from the parish to fill their "font." Children should keep the "font" in their bedroom to remind them to begin and end their day with the Sign of the Cross, using the holy water as a reminder of their Baptism.

---

* Whenever working with paints, have children spread newspaper on work surfaces and wear paint shirts, smocks, or other protective clothing.

Light of Christ Card

During Lent, we prepare to renew our baptismal promises. We renew our life of faith. This craft reminds children to thank those who helped them to grow in faith.

Supplies needed:

white, yellow, and peach card stock
3 1/2" square pieces of foam sheet
craft scissors with patterned edges
glue stick
pearl glitter glue

Directions:

1. Have children fold peach card stock in half to form card.

2. Cut along the open edges using scissors with patterned edges.

3. Cut candlestick out of white card stock and a flame out of yellow card stock, using templates provided.

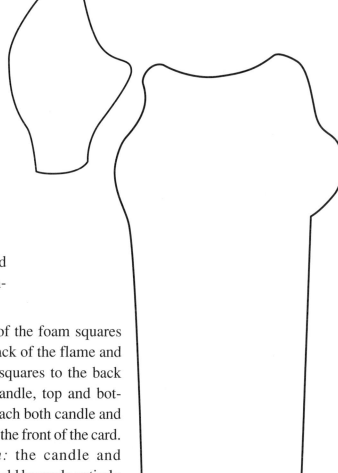

4. Glue 1 of the foam squares to the back of the flame and 2 foam squares to the back of the candle, top and bottom. Attach both candle and flame to the front of the card. (*Option:* the candle and flame could be made entirely out of foam sheets.)

5. Decorate the candle with glitter glue. Allow to dry.

6. On the inside of the card, children can write a message to their godparents or someone in the parish or school who has helped them to grow in faith. The message could be as simple as, "Thank you for sharing your light of faith with me." Have them mail or deliver their cards.

Robed in White

Easy

During Lent, as we reflect on our baptismal promises, we re-commit to avoiding sin, believing in God and his love for us shown in Jesus, and living in the community of the Catholic Church. This craft project reminds children that the white garments of Baptism signify the new life we received in the sacrament.

Teacher/Parent Preparation:

A week in advance, send home with each child a paper asking the parent(s) for the date on which the child was baptized.

Supplies needed:

8 1/2" x 11" white foam sheet

craft scissors with patterned edges

hole punch

fabric paints, pens, or markers*

paint shirts or smocks

newspaper

Directions:

1. Have children spread newspaper over work surfaces and put on their paint shirts.

2. Each child can use the template provided on page 67 to trace their "robe" onto a white foam sheet.

3. Cut out robes, using regular scissors. Trim along edges of sleeves and lower edge of robe using special craft scissors with patterned edges.

4. Using fabric paints, pens, or markers, children can mark the following on their robe:

a cross near the neckline; their baptismal name near the hemline; the date they were baptized above cross; present date below the cross. (Be sure to allow plenty of time for robe to dry completely.) Writing these two dates acknowledges not only the date of their Baptism, but also reminds them that we daily renew our baptismal promises as we continue to live lives of faith.

5. Hang the robes in your classroom/home as a reminder of their Baptism and the baptismal promises we are called to keep.

"And when you were baptized, it was as though you had put on Christ in the same way you put on new clothes" (Galatians 3:27).

---

* *Whenever working with paints, have children spread newspaper on work surfaces and wear paint shirts, smocks, or other protective clothing.*

Reflection

When mankind was estranged from him by disobedience, God our Savior made a plan for raising us from our fall and restoring us to friendship with himself. According to this plan Christ came in the flesh, he showed us the Gospel way of life, he suffered, died on the cross, was buried, and rose from the dead. He did this so that we could be saved by imitation of him and recover our original status as sons of God by adoption.

St. Basil

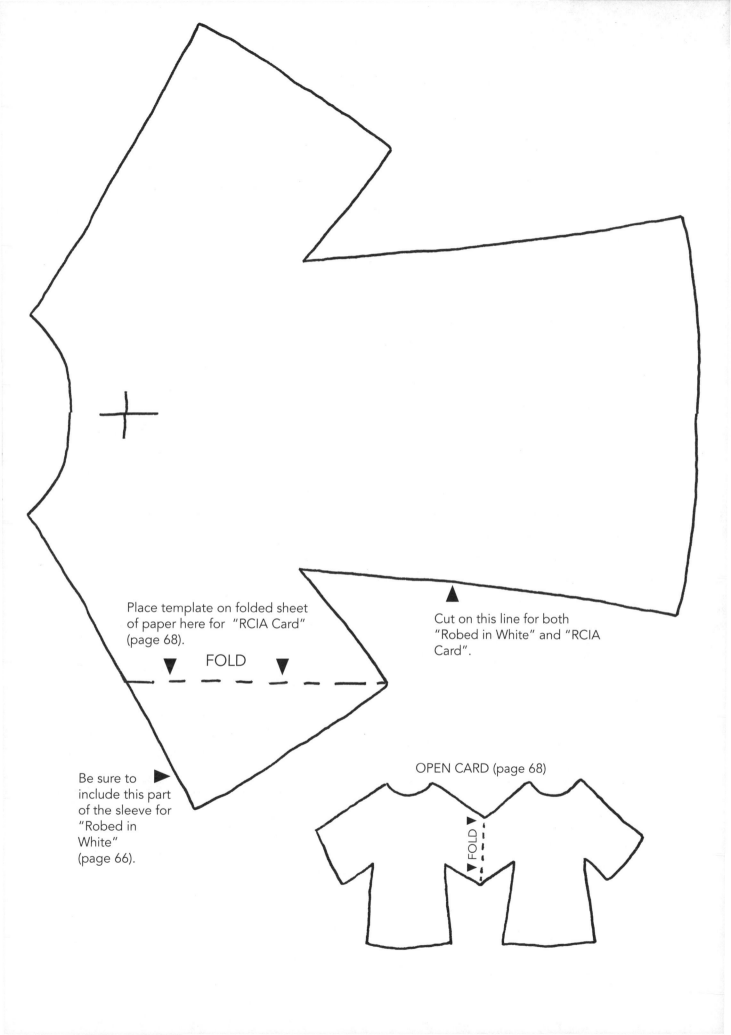

Place template on folded sheet of paper here for "RCIA Card" (page 68).

▼ FOLD ▼

Cut on this line for both "Robed in White" and "RCIA Card".

Be sure to include this part of the sleeve for "Robed in White" (page 66).

OPEN CARD (page 68)

FOLD

Card for RCIA and RCIC Candidates

During Lent, RCIA and RCIC candidates are busy making their final preparations for the sacraments of initiation: Baptism, Confirmation, and the Eucharist. Cards and letters of encouragement help them to know that the Church community is supporting them in their journey of faith. Help children participate in the process by making cards for the "elect."

Teacher/Parent Preparation:

Obtain from the rectory the names of the "candidates" for entrance into the Church from the parish.

You may need to explain the RCIA and RCIC programs to children. The following explanation may help:

During Lent, adults and older children who have not yet been baptized into the Catholic Church but who want to belong to the Catholic Church make their final preparations to receive the sacraments of Initiation (Baptism, Confirmation, and the Eucharist) at the Easter Vigil Mass. Adults are involved in special classes, known as the RCIA program (Rite of Christian Initiation for Adults). Older children participate in similar classes known as RCIC (Rite of Christian Initiation for Children). They are called "candidates" because they are not yet a part of the Church. Because we are already members of the Church community, we help to welcome these new members through prayerful support and cards or letters of encouragement.

Supplies needed:

11" x 17" white construction paper or computer paper

scissors

craft scissors with patterned edges

markers, pens, crayons

template on page 67

Directions:

1. Have children fold white construction paper in half widthwise. (The folded paper will form an 11 by 8 1/2-inch rectangle.)

2. Using the template on page 67, trace the "robe" on the folded paper. The left side of the template should be even with the fold.

3. Cut out the robe-shaped card.

4. Decorate the front of the cards with a cross, writing the year below the cross and the name of one of the RCIA or RCIC candidates across the bottom of the card. Trim the bottom of the card using patterned scissors.

5. Write a note of encouragement to the candidates inside the card.

6. Cards should be collected and given to the coordinator of the RCIA/RCIC program for distribution to the "elect."

Reflection

It is true. If you believe that Jesus Christ is Lord and that God has raised him from the dead, you will be saved. Jesus on the cross on Calvary welcomed the thief to Paradise. He will welcome you also.

St. Cyril of Jerusalem

Baptism

Dear Parent(s),

During the Lenten season, we will be focusing on different aspects of Lent: its meaning, its symbols, its customs, and its traditions. Each week, your child will bring home Family Take-Home Pages, which are filled with activities that reinforce what we are discussing and learning in class. These Take-Home Pages are theme based and divided into three sections: Warm-Up Exercises, Getting Started, and Putting It into Practice. The theme for this week of Lent is Baptism.

During Lent adults who are interested in joining the faith are busy preparing to receive the sacraments of initiation, which include Baptism, Confirmation, and the Eucharist. For those who have already been baptized, Lent is a time when we prepare to renew our baptismal promises on Easter. It is a time when we recommit to those promises of faith. May the activities suggested in these pages provide you with additional tools for nurturing your child's faith.

Warm-Up Exercises...

Gather the family around the Lenten candle. Have one member of the family light the candle and another read from Scripture. Then follow with a family discussion.

A reading from John 3:1–6

There was a man named Nicodemus who was a Pharisee and a Jewish leader. One night he went to Jesus and said, "Sir, we know that God has sent you to teach us. You could not work these miracles, unless´ God were with you."

Jesus replied, "I tell you for certain that you must be born from above before you can see God's kingdom!"

Nicodemus asked, "How can a grown man ever be born a second time?"

Jesus answered, "I tell you for certain that before you can get into God's kingdom, you must be born not only by water, but by the Spirit. Humans give life to their children. Yet only God's Spirit can change you into a child of God."

Follow with a discussion about the Baptism of each family member. Invite family members to share their memories of those special days. Try to remember as many of the details as you can. Were different members of the family baptized in different parishes? Recall the name(s) of the priest(s) who baptized the different members of your family. Why did you choose the godparents you chose? Who celebrated these special days with your family? Were any family members baptized as adults? If so, share their conversion story with your children. Why is Baptism such a wonderful gift? Pull out any photos or videos of your children's Baptisms.

— 69 —

Say a prayer of thanks for the gift of Baptism. And say a special prayer for the priest(s), godparents, family, and friends who celebrated the sacrament of Baptism with you.

Getting Started...

During Lent we prepare to renew our Baptismal promises; we examine how well we are upholding the promises we made, or the promises our godparents made for us. As we grow in faith, we continually renew these commitments to our faith. Take a few moments now to renew those promises as a family baptized in faith. Have different members of the family take turns asking the questions. The rest of the family responds: I do.

Do you reject Satan and all his works and all his empty promises?

Do you believe in God the Father almighty, creator of heaven and earth?

Do you believe in Jesus Christ, his only Son, our Lord, who was born of the virgin Mary, was crucified, died, and was buried, rose from the dead, and is now seated at the right hand of the Father?

Do you believe in the Holy Spirit, the Lord, the giver of life, who proceeds from the Father and Son?

Do you believe in the holy catholic Church, the communion of saints, the forgiveness of sins, the resurrection of the body, and life everlasting?

After renewing your baptismal promises, hold hands and thank God for the gift of faith.

Putting It into Practice...

Does your family know someone who will be baptized soon? This person could be a relative, a personal friend, or one of the candidates in your parish's RCIA or RCIC program. How will your family welcome this person into the Church? How will your family continue to support him/her in faith? Brainstorm about ways your family can support this person, and then put those ideas into action. Here are some suggestions to get you started:

Make and send bookmarks that can be used in a Bible. Include verses from Scripture that relate to Baptism (John 3:5, Luke 3:16, Titus 3:5, Romans 6:3–7, Acts 2: 38).

Make and send letters of welcome and congratulations.

Make and send cards of encouragement.

Pray for that person.

Invite that person for supper.

Send notes telling that person that your family is praying for him/her.

Invite that person and his/her family to go to Mass with yours.

Invite that person and his/her family to attend other church functions with your family.

"You must encourage one another each day" (Hebrews 3:13).

> Traditions create memories. Memories enrich our lives. Traditions also help us pass on valuable lessons to our children.

During Lent, we reflect on our baptismal promises. At the Easter Mass, we will renew the commitment we made at our Baptism.

For candidates of the RCIA and RCIC programs, Lent provides a time of final preparation for receiving the sacraments of initiation. The Church community will soon be celebrating with great joy these new members of the Church at the Easter Vigil Mass.

Many Catholic families celebrate the day of a child's Baptism with great gusto. Family members, neighbors, and friends help the family celebrate this special occasion. The baby, all adorned in white, is the center of attention. White is the customary color for the baptismal outfit. Baptism purifies us from all sins—original and personal—and makes the baptized person a new creature, an adopted child of God, who is a partaker of the divine nature, a member of the Body of Christ, and a temple of the Holy Spirit. The baptized person becomes a member of the Church and belongs forever to Jesus, who died and rose for us.

As a symbol of new life through Baptism, some families (and parishes) make simple white garments for the "newly baptized" member of the Church. This garment slips over the baby's head. There are no seams. They're easy to make.* Their hems can be machine or hand-stitched. Non-sewers and non-crafters can make these garments from felt, so there's no need to stitch hems. The

only embellishments on the garment are a tiny cross, embroidered near the neckline, and the child's name and date of Baptism embroidered near the hemline.

These white garments make perfect keepsakes of your child's Baptism. And they make thoughtful gifts from godparents to godchild. You could make several outfits as gifts for babies who will be baptized in the near future in your parish. If possible take your children to attend these baptismal celebrations.

The pattern is on pages 72–73.

Supplies needed:

1/3 yard of 45"-wide white felt

straight pins (for pinning pattern to felt)

embroidery needle (wide-eye)

embroidery floss (suggested colors: red for cross; blue for boy's names; pink for girl's names)

fabric pinking shears or scissors

Directions:

1. Trace and cut out pattern on pages 72–73.

2. Lay felt flat on table. It should measure 12 by 45 inches. Pin pattern to felt and cut.

3. Cut slit in neckline as shown on pattern to allow garment to fit over baby's head.

4. Embroider a small cross near the front neckline, using 3 strands of embroidery floss (see diagram).

5. Embroider the child's name and baptismal date on the front, near hemline of gown, using 3 strands of embroidery floss.

---

* The supplies call for felt rather than fabric so that the project is easier to do.

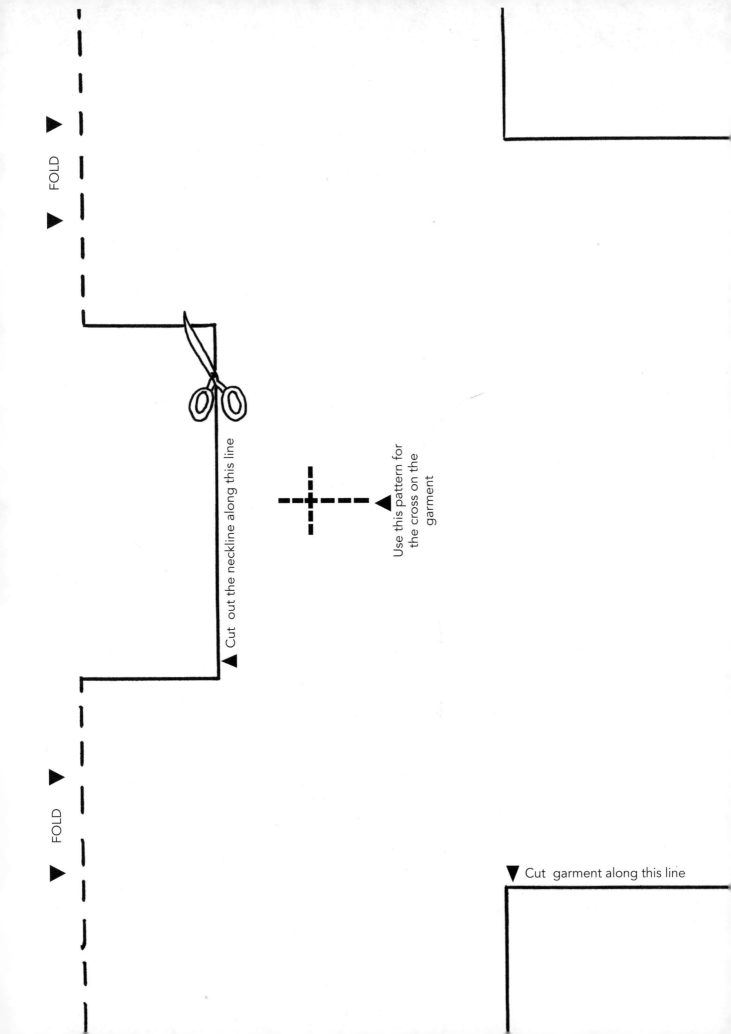

FOLD

FOLD

Cut out the neckline along this line

Use this pattern for the cross on the garment

Cut garment along this line

Pattern for white garment

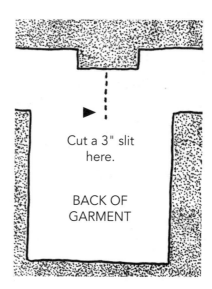

Cut a 3" slit here.

BACK OF GARMENT

Cross, Death, and Resurrection

Each week during the Lenten and Easter seasons, we will be focusing on a different theme. The theme for this week of Lent is the Cross, Death, and Resurrection.

A variety of activities is provided so you can choose those that best fit your children's needs. Some activities call for quiet reflection and others involve group discussions. Some require advance planning because you will need to gather supplies for craft projects. You may want to flip to the back of the book to the reproducible pages to see if there are any additional materials you might want to use.

Lent is a time when we examine how well we are living our faith. It is a time when we reflect more deeply on Jesus' suffering, crucifixion, and death. But we also look forward to the promise of his resurrection!

For those following a lectionary-based catechesis, this theme corresponds to the readings for the second Sunday of Lent.

Week-at-a-Glance

Reflection

Lent is a time of intense prayer and extended praise; it is a time of penance and fasting. But along with prayer and fasting, the liturgy invites us to fill our day with works of charity. The image before us is one of a banquet, the symbol of the heavenly Father's gracious providence toward all men and women. Everyone must be able to partake of it. For this reason, the Lenten practices of fasting and almsgiving not only express personal asceticism, but also have an important social and community function: they recall the need to "convert" the model of development to a more just distribution of goods, so that everyone can live in dignity and, at the same time, creation itself may be protected.

John Paul II

———————

Tell souls where they are to look for solace; that is, in the tribunal of Mercy. There the greatest miracles take place [and] are incessantly repeated. To avail oneself of this miracle, it is not necessary to go on a great pilgrimage or to carry out some external ceremony; it suffices to come with faith to the feet of my representative and to reveal to him one's misery, and the miracle of Divine Mercy will be fully demonstrated.

Jesus to St. Faustina

———————

Cross of Christ, to you be praise. We hail you in every age, from you there spring power and strength, in you our victory!

John Paul II

Help your children to focus on the words of the cross with their own words of praise.

Gather children around the prayer table and light the Lenten candle (see page 11). Stand a crucifix on the table, too.

Say to the children: During Lent we remember how Jesus came looking for us—all of us who had fallen into a deep pit of sin and darkness. Jesus came to pull us out of death and reinstate us in life. (Talk about the Good Shepherd who searches for his lost sheep.) Jesus came to heal and save us by loving us.

When we make the Sign of the Cross, we remember God's great love for us. We say, "In the name of the Father, and of the Son, and of the Holy Spirit. Amen." The Sign of the Cross is a "simple prayer of praise."

For today's prayer experience, let's think about the words we pray when we make the Sign of the Cross. Now let's come up with additional words we can add to that simple prayer of praise. It might sound something like this: "In the name of the Father, who created all good things; and of the Son, who died and rose for us; and of the Holy Spirit, who is with us forever and always. Amen."

Explain to children that they should make the Sign of the Cross slowly and deliberately, thinking about the words they are praying. It is a gesture of reverence and praise.

Give children time to think of a simple prayer of praise. Ask them to share their prayers with each other.

Choose one of their suggestions for a simple prayer of praise (or combine a few suggestions) and under the title, "Simple Prayer of Praise," write the prayer on the chalkboard or on an index card. Then pray the prayer together as a class/family.

Remember to pray this "Simple Prayer of Praise" often throughout the week.

the Challenge

By Carol A. Grund

The fifteen-mile race was a challenge,
but the real challenge was deciding how
badly they wanted to win it.

Illustrated by
Luanne Marten

"37…37…37…"

Brandon had been staring at that number for so long, it was like a refrain in his head.

He'd even started pedaling his bike to its rhythm.

The 37 was pinned to the back of his friend Josh's WMLQ

T-shirt. That was the radio station sponsoring today's bike race. It had started at their business office in town and would

Book

end at their transmitter tower, fifteen miles away.

Although Brandon and Josh liked bike riding anyway, it was the prize that inspired them to sign up for this race—kids with the fastest time in their age brackets would win CD players and a big stack of CDs. The boys had figured it would take a whole lot of lawn mowing to earn money for that kind of prize. Now, wearing their official WMLQ shirts and entry tags, they'd already covered the first five miles.

"Checkpoint ahead!" Josh called over his shoulder.

The boys signed in, and then quickly started off again. If they were going to beat the times of every thirteen-year-old in the race, they couldn't afford to waste a single second!

This time Brandon took the lead, and, before long, the route took them along paved country roads. Brandon noticed a hand-lettered sign in front of one house: *Fresh Strawberries*. It made him hungry. "Too bad we can't stop," he called to Josh.

A collie dog in that same yard had stopped chasing a squirrel to follow them. He barked out a friendly greeting.

"Go on, boy," Brandon called. "Go back now!"

"Move over," Josh advised, "there's a car coming."

They were both on the gravel shoulder when they heard it—a screeching sound followed by a sickening thud.

Suddenly the car accelerated and sped off.

Brandon turned to look back. His stomach clenched up as he realized what had happened—the playful collie now lay still and silent by the side of the road.

"Josh!" he yelled, turning his bike around.

He tossed his bike and helmet to the grass and crouched down beside the dog. "He's alive," he said, "but his leg is bleeding."

Josh bent down to look, but backed away quickly, his face a grayish color.

"Someone will come along who knows what to do," he said. "I think we should go."

Brandon looked down the road in both directions. No cars were in sight now, but Josh was probably right—one would be along any minute. An adult would be able to help the dog much better than they could. And they hadn't lost much time yet.

"Okay," he agreed.

He was reaching for his bike when he nearly slipped in some blood on the grass. Brandon knew that humans could go into shock from blood loss—he wondered if that happened to animals, too.

Help me, he thought. *I don't know what to do.*

He hadn't really meant it as a prayer, but an answer popped into his head just the same. It was another prayer he had learned from his first grade teacher years ago: *Dear God, let me do what I can, where I am, with what I have.*

He pulled off his T-shirt and began wrapping it tightly around the dog's leg. "You go ahead without me," he said. "I'm going to try to find the owner."

"But—" Josh started to protest, then changed his mind. "No, you stay with him," he said, then took off running toward the house.

The dog looked up with sad brown eyes.

"It's all right," Brandon told him, stroking the golden head. "You'll be all right."

Some bike riders passed by, but no cars appeared. It seemed like an eternity since Josh had gone. Brandon was afraid the collie's life was slipping away right in his arms.

"Hold on, boy," he whispered.

Finally Josh appeared, trailed by a gray-haired woman. Brandon saw tears in her eyes as she knelt beside the collie. Her callused hands were gentle as she touched the matted fur.

"Oh, Toby," she said. The dog's ears twitched at the sound of her voice.

She turned to Brandon and Josh. "Can you help me get him into the car?"

Just minutes later, the car was on its way to the veterinarian's office, with Toby wrapped in a blanket on the back seat. Their hearts still pounding, Brandon and Josh watched it go.

"I'm sorry about the race," Brandon said, his voice a little shaky, "but I—"

"No, you were right," Josh interrupted. "I was just scared, I guess. Plus, I really wanted to win."

"Me, too," Brandon said, strapping on his helmet.

But both boys knew the race was over for them. The fun and excitement were gone. Silently, they turned their bikes around and headed home.

At dinner, Brandon pushed his food around the plate. It seemed like his stomach would never feel right again. He could still see those brown eyes looking at him.

"I know you feel badly," his mother said, "but you boys did all you could for that dog."

"We almost didn't," Brandon said miserably. "We wanted to let someone else handle it so we wouldn't have to."

The phone rang in the kitchen, and Brandon's father got up to get it.

"I'll drive you back there," his mother offered, "if you think you could find the house again."

"I know I could," Brandon answered, "but what if—"

His father returned, handing the phone to Brandon. "It's for you."

"Hello," said a woman's voice. "This is Eleanor Tollman, Toby's owner. I wanted to let you know that Toby's going to be fine. His leg was broken and needed stitches, but the vet said you saved his life by putting that tourniquet on. I'm so grateful, Brandon. Toby is very special to me."

The knot in Brandon's stomach started to loosen.

"That's great!" he told her. Then he realized something. "But…I never told you my name. How did you find me?"

"You left a big clue behind," she explained. "Your shirt had a number on the back. The people at the radio station were kind enough to give me your name when I explained what happened. I wanted to give you a reward."

"No, really, that's okay," Brandon protested. "Toby's

a cool dog. But…well, maybe Josh and I could visit him sometime?"

"We'd love it," Mrs. Tollman said. "And if you won't accept a reward, would you consider a job? I need some help picking these strawberries. I'd pay you boys, and you could see Toby then."

"Wow, thanks!" Brandon answered, smiling for the first time since the accident happened.

"Then it's settled," she said. "I'll just need to ask your parents' permission. Maybe they could join us afterward for strawberry shortcake. How does that sound?"

Brandon's stomach growled. Suddenly he was starving.

"Delicious!" he answered. Still smiling, he handed the phone back to his father and picked up his fork.

Reprinted from My Friend: The Catholic Magazine for Kids, *Pauline Books & Media, 50 Saint Pauls Avenue, Boston, MA 02130.*
www.myfriendmagazine.com

Discussion Starters for Grades K–3

- If you were in the same situation as Brandon and Josh, would you quit the race to help? Why or why not?

- What do you think the boys learned from this experience?

They had to give up something they really wanted—to win the bicycle race—in order to take care of the dog who needed their help. Jesus also gave up something he loved—his own life—in order to take care of us who needed his help.

- What are some times when you have had to give up something you really wanted in order to help or serve others?

Discussion Starters for Grades 4–8

- Did you ever want to participate in a contest but something prevented you from competing? What type of competition was it? What kept you from participating?

- How did you feel about that?

- If you found yourself in the same situation as Brandon and Josh, would you stop to help an animal? Why, why not?

- Would you stop to help a fellow racer who takes a spill? Why, why not?

- What parable does this story remind you of?

Read the parable of the Good Samaritan from the Gospel of Luke (10:25–37).

- How are the two situations similar?

Then read the hymn to Christ in the Letter of Paul to the Philippians (2:1–11).

Paul is saying that Jesus cared about us the way he cared about himself. So he didn't hold on to the status of being God, but became a man and served us, and even died for us on a cross. Now Jesus is in the highest place and his name is honored above all others.

Either play a video of the life of Jesus (the segment of the crucifixion and resurrection) or play a contemporary Christian song about Jesus giving his life for us.

- What are ways that you can care for others the way you would care for yourself, to put others' needs first instead of your own? We belong now to Christ. We are called to act like him by serving not ourselves but others.

Have the children express what this means for them through prayer, song, or art.

Reflection

This Lent, can you forgive and leave behind the burden of resentment and nourished hurts you have carried around through the years? Can you hold out reconciliation and be the first to forgive and to ask for forgiveness?

Christine Vladimiroff, OSB

The death of the Lord our God should not be a cause of shame for us; rather, it should be our greatest hope, our greatest glory. In taking upon himself the death that he found in us, he has most faithfully promised to give us life in him, such as we cannot have of ourselves.

St. Augustine

Sock Talk and Lettered Laces

This craft project helps children to proclaim their faith in yet a different way!

Supplies needed:

fabric paints, fabric or permanent markers*

white cotton socks, pre-washed (1 set per child)

white flat shoelaces, pre-washed (1 set per child)

cardboard (to fit inside sock)

paint shirts or smocks

newspaper

Directions for Sock Talk:

1. Have children spread newspaper over work surfaces and put on their paint shirts.

2. Have children determine how they will wear their painted socks: pulled up or cuffed. If pulled up, have them place a piece of cardboard into each sock (to keep paints/markers from soaking through). If cuffed, turn socks inside out and then place cardboard inside. They will also need to write their message along the edge of the sock. It will look upside down, but when they cuff their socks, the message will be fine. (See illustration.)

3. Smooth all wrinkles before printing proclamations of faith with paints/markers on socks. Follow directions on fabric markers. Only print on one side of the socks; then allow those to dry before printing on the other side.

4. Choose from proclamations listed or come up with your own.

Directions for Lettered Laces:

1. Have children spread newspaper over work surfaces and wear paint shirts to protect their clothes.

2. Spread shoelaces flat onto table.

3. Using permanent fabric markers, print proclamation on the ends of laces that hang after laced. Let dry. Lace shoes.

Proclamations:

I walk the Lord's way.

Jesus Christ gives me life.

Jesus came and now I have life.

I'm never alone.

Believe in Jesus. Have eternal life.

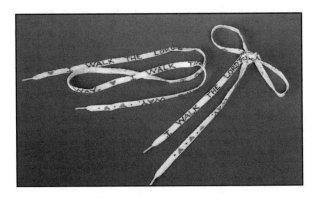

---

* Whenever working with paints, have children spread newspaper on work surfaces and wear paint shirts or other protective clothing.

The Lent–Easter Book

Tees Please

Easy

Another fun, fabric paint project to help kids proclaim the faith they're proud of!

Supplies needed:

cotton tee shirt, pre-washed (1 per child)

cardboard (1 per child, the size of the tee shirt)

fabric paints*

fabric markers

pencil

paint shirts or smocks

newspaper

Directions:

1. Have children spread newspaper over work surfaces and put on their paint shirts.

2. Lay tee shirts on table/desk tops and slide a piece of cardboard between the front and back of the tee shirt to keep paints from leaking through.

3. Have children pencil their proclamation onto their shirts and then apply paints or markers over the pencil lines. See suggested proclamations.

4. Let paints dry, then remove cardboard.

Proclamations:

Never turn your back on Jesus.

Yes! I believe!

Stand up and be counted.

Jesus heals.

---

* Whenever working with paints, have children spread newspaper on work surfaces and wear paint shirts, smocks, or other protective clothing.

Reflection

"Repent and believe in the Gospel." This invitation, which we find at the beginning of Jesus' preaching, is appropriate for the Lenten season, a time dedicated in a special way to conversion and renewal, to prayer, to fasting, and to works of charity. In recalling the experience of the chosen people, we too set out as if it were to retrace the journey that Israel made across the desert to the Promised Land. We too will reach our goal; after these weeks of penance, we too will experience the joy of Easter. Our eyes, purified by prayer and penance, will be able to behold with greater clarity the face of the living God, to whom we make our own pilgrimage on the paths of earthly life.

John Paul II

Cross of Twine

Help children focus on the Way of the Cross with this craft that combines audio and visual art. While children are busy applying twine to their cardboard crosses, play a Lenten CD, or read a reflection about one of the stations (see pages 143–158).

Supplies needed:

1/4"-thick craft foam sheets or cardboard (corrugated works best), 8 1/2" x 11" (1 per child)

twine or thin jute

white glue

scissors

pencils

newspaper

Directions:

1. Have children spread newspaper over work surfaces.

2. Have children cut out a cross from craft foam sheets or corrugated cardboard.

3. Draw free-flowing patterns on the crosses.

4. Fill in the designs using twine and glue. The twine should be applied to form repeated, concentric shapes. (See photo.) Use varying widths and thicknesses of twine to form interesting designs.

5. When glue dries, turn cross over. On back of cross glue a "loop" of twine covered by a 1-inch square of cardboard. When dry, the cross is ready to hang on the wall.

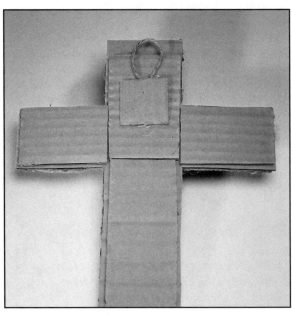

"Then Jesus said to his disciples: 'If any of you want to be my followers, you must forget about yourself. You must take up your cross and follow me'" (Matthew 16:24).

Easter Card Made with Buttons

Eggs and flowers are traditional symbols for new life. Help children to make cards that reflect the true meaning of this season with egg-shaped cards decorated with a floral bouquet or cross. The cards are a perfect way to send prayerful greetings to family and friends.

Supplies needed:

card stock, various pastel colors (2 per child)

scissors   glue

pencils, markers   tape

craft scissors with patterned edges

buttons, different sizes, shapes, and colors (3 per child for flowers; 11 per child for cross)

green embroidery floss

embroidery needle (wide eye)

Directions:

1. Have children select 2 different colors of card stock.

2. Fold 1 of the pieces of card stock in half to form a card. Cut the other piece of card stock in half. This half will be used for the "egg." Trace an oval along the edge of the card stock. (See photo.)

3. To make a bouquet of flowers, sketch stems and leaves on the oval piece of card stock. To make a cross, stitch seven buttons in a vertical line. Stitch 4 more to form the cross bar.

4. Demonstrate how to thread needle and stitch stems and leaves, using 3 strands of embroidery floss. (Knot one end of the floss and start stitching from the back of the oval, poking the needle through to the front so that knot is hidden on the back of the card stock.)

5. Stitch leaves and stems.

6. When finished with stems and leaves, secure the other end of the floss on the back of the card by knotting it. Trim excess floss.

7. Thread needle with more floss, knot the end, and stitch the buttons in place for the "flowers."

8. To attach "egg" to card, "roll" 4 pieces of tape, attach tape to back of "egg," and press "egg" to card.

9. Write prayerful messages for family or friends inside cards.

Alternative for younger children:

Have children glue buttons to egg and draw stems and leaves with markers.

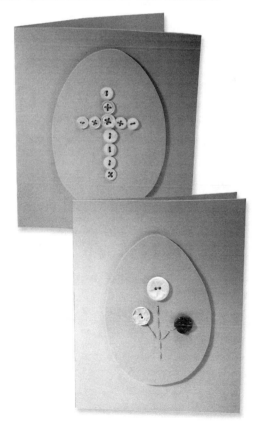

Quill Cross

The cross is a symbol of Jesus' ultimate gift of love for us, his willingness to die and rise so that we could have new life in him. Help your children to form beautiful crosses with paper, toothpicks, and glue.

Anyone can quill. It simply requires wrapping narrow strips of paper around toothpicks to form little "coils" for making intricate, lacey designs. By pinching, squeezing, or creasing these coils, you alter their shapes. (See samples on page 85.) By combining a variety of coiled shapes, the final design can form a one-of-a-kind work of art.

Supplies needed:

- 1/8" strips, 11 1/2" long of white construction paper (minimum of 24 strips per child, 28 is ideal)
- round toothpicks (1 per child)
- clear-drying craft glue
- newspapers
- thin string, floss or quilting thread for hanging
- Alternative for younger children: use white pompoms (24 or 28 pompoms per child—3/8"-diameter pompoms are easier to glue) and white paper

Directions:

1. Have children spread newspaper over work surfaces.

2. Begin by winding 1 strip of white paper around a toothpick, making sure to wrap the paper tightly for the first few times.

3. Hold the paper with one hand, while turning the toothpick with the other. Children should hold paper between their fingers just tight enough to keep the coil from slipping off the toothpick.  They should continue rolling the paper until the entire strip is used.

4. If a tight coil is desired, when children have finished rolling their strip of paper, they should glue the end to the coil before removing it from toothpick. If a loose coil is desired, allow the coil to unwind to the desired effect, then glue the end of the strip to the coil and remove coil from toothpick.

5. A basic cross requires a minimum of 24 white coils. To make a more elaborate design, additional coils are needed.

6. Have children arrange coils in the shape of a cross. (See photo.)

7. Before gluing the edges of the coils together, children should determine if they want "round" coils, "square" coils, etc. (See page

85.) These shapes can be formed by pinching and squeezing the coils.

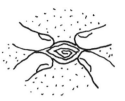 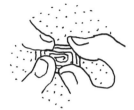

8. Once children have determined their designs, they should glue all the coils together using toothpicks to apply dabs of glue where coils meet.

9. Once glue has dried, thread thin string through the center of the top coil for hanging.

Alternative for younger children:

Have children glue pompoms in the shape of a cross to white paper and then trim paper when glue is dry. Poke a hole at the top of the cross and tie a loop for hanging with thin string.

 Tight coils—Roll paper strip tightly on toothpick, then glue end of coil in place before removing coil from toothpick.

Loose coil—Roll a tight coil, then remove it from the toothpick and allow it to unwind or expand a little before gluing the end of the coil in place.

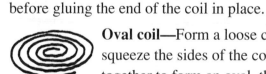 **Oval coil**—Form a loose coil, squeeze the sides of the coil together to form an oval, then glue end of coil in place.

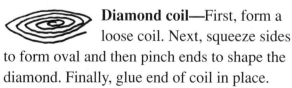 **Diamond coil**—First, form a loose coil. Next, squeeze sides to form oval and then pinch ends to shape the diamond. Finally, glue end of coil in place.

 Square coil—Form a loose coil, then shape into a diamond by pinching the ends. Next, pinch

the sides again, forming a square. Glue end of coil in place.

 Rectangle coil—Form a loose coil, then squeeze the sides to form an oval. Next, pinch 2 corners at both ends of the oval to form the rectangle. Glue end of coil in place.

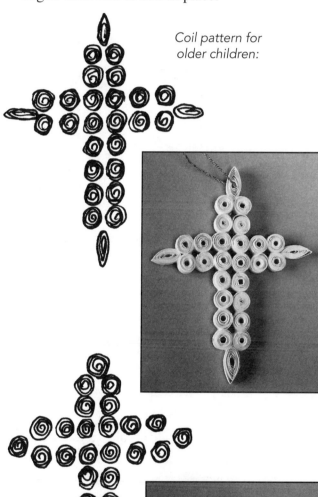

Coil pattern for older children:

Pompom pattern for younger children:

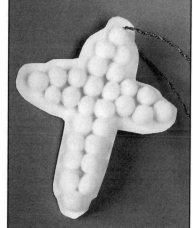

Hot Cross Buns

Have fun with your children in the kitchen while making delicious buns that display the Sign of the Cross. Before enjoying these delicious treats, thank God for the gift of his Son.

Ingredients:

Dough:

1 pkg. fast-acting yeast

1/4 cup warm water

1 cup milk, scalded

1/2 cup margarine

1/2 tsp. cinnamon

3/4 tsp. salt

1/2 cup sugar

3/4 cup raisins

1 egg

4 cups flour

Icing:

1 cup confectioners' sugar

dash of salt   milk

Directions:

1. In large mixing bowl, dissolve yeast according to directions on the package in the 1/4 cup of water.

2. Place milk in microwavable dish and cook on high for 3 minutes.

3. Remove bowl from microwave and add salt, sugar, cinnamon, and margarine to milk.

4. When milk mixture is lukewarm, add to dissolved yeast the egg, 1 cup of flour, and raisins, and mix well.

5. Then add the remaining flour, mixing well.

6. On floured board, knead dough until smooth.

7. Place dough into greased bowl and cover with a clean kitchen towel. Let dough rise for an hour.

8. Remove cover. Punch down dough.

9. Tear off bits of dough and form twelve buns; place on greased cookie sheet, close together. Let rise for about 30 minutes.

10. With a butter knife, cut a cross-shape on the top of each bun. Bake for 15–20 minutes at 375 degrees or until golden brown.

11. Prepare the icing: Mix confectioners' sugar, a dash of salt, and just enough milk to form a thick consistency.

12. When buns cool, fill crosses with icing.

Reflection

The season of Lent forms us to share in the mystery of Christ's death and resurrection.

Katie Grace

The Lent–Easter Book

Cross, Death, and Resurrection

Dear Parent(s),

During the Lenten season, we will be focusing on different aspects of Lent: its meaning, its symbols, its customs, and its traditions. Each week, your child will bring home Family Take-Home Pages, which are filled with activities that reinforce what we are discussing and learning in class. These Take-Home Pages are theme-based and divided into three sections: Warm-Up Exercises, Getting Started, and Putting It into Practice. The theme for this week of Lent is the Cross, Death, and Resurrection. May the activities suggested in these pages provide you with additional tools for nurturing your child's faith.

Warm-Up Exercises...

Gather the family around the Lenten candle. Have one member of the family light the candle and another read from Scripture. Then follow with a family discussion.

A reading from the first letter of Peter 2:24

Christ carried the burden of our sins. He was nailed to the cross, so that we would stop sinning and start living right. By his cuts and bruises you are healed.

After sharing this passage with your family, reflect on it together by using the following questions.

Even though Jesus died on the cross more than 2,000 years ago, he died for the sins of all people throughout all of history. How often do we thank Jesus for dying on the cross so that we would be saved from the power of sin and death?

How do we show Jesus we're grateful for his tremendous gift of love? Through our prayers? Our words? Our actions? How central is this to our life?

How do we share the Good News of salvation with others?

Getting Started...

Have a third family member read this passage from Scripture.

A reading from John 19:25

Jesus' mother stood beside the cross with her sister and Mary the wife of Clopas. Mary Magdalene was standing there, too. When Jesus saw his mother and his favorite disciple with her, he said to his mother, "This man is now your son." Then he said to the disciple, "She is now your mother." From then on, that disciple took her into his own home.

After reading this passage from Scripture, have another family discussion. Here are some questions to get you started:

Are you willing, like Mary, to stand by Jesus today? Share some examples that prove that you are.

Think about some of the decisions you've made recently that show that you want to follow Jesus. Share these with your family.

Think of some things you've wanted to do but hesitated to do because you thought your friends wouldn't understand. These things could be as public as participating in the March for Life or making the Sign of the Cross and saying grace before meals when dining at a restaurant. It could be more subtle such as remembering to say, "Oh, gosh!" instead of, "Oh, God!" What's keeping you from speaking or acting the way God wants you to?

In the early days of the Church, Christians were persecuted for their faith. There are people in different parts of the world who are still persecuted for their faith. If you were arrested or persecuted for being a follower of Jesus and for living your faith, would you still choose to follow Jesus and to live your faith? Why or why not?

Now take a moment to pray as a family that God will give you the courage to live the faith that you profess.

Putting It into Practice...

This activity will help your family realize that even a little help can make a big difference!

Supplies needed:

bucket with handle

canned goods

broomstick

Directions:

Fill a bucket with canned goods. Ask a family member to carry the bucket to another room. (It should be difficult.) Ask someone else to help. With two people carrying the load by the handle, it should be somewhat easier. Slide the broomstick under the handle and have three or four people carry the load to make it lighter.

Explain that some people carry tremendous loads; some carry their loads or

"crosses" alone. Sometimes we carry "crosses." But we don't have to carry them alone. Jesus helps us. And we, as caring Christians, can physically help carry each other's loads. We can also join others in prayerful support. Both are helpful. Both are needed. Simon of Cyrene helped carry Jesus' cross.

Now have your family think of someone who is carrying a heavy load (or cross) and discuss ways that you can help carry his or her "cross" or ease the burden. It can be a family member, a neighbor, a relative, a friend, someone from school, church, or work. Then make it a family effort to do something to help.

Reflection

Lent is not a time when we regretfully step back from all the fun and joy we have in life to enthusiastically pretend we are good Christians by starting a diet. Lent is a time when we remember that God invites us to true joy. God is love. All our preoccupations with anything less than what God intends for us is illusion.

Sr. Kathryn James, FSP

Eucharistic Adoration

Though many Catholics attend Mass more frequently during Lent, Eucharistic adoration provides another opportunity for us to be in the presence of Jesus, our Savior and Lord. Individuals, families and school children find Eucharistic adoration another meaningful way to reflect on Christ's passion, death, and resurrection during Lent and Easter, as well as throughout the year.

In the celebration of the Eucharist, Christ becomes present under the form of bread and wine, and we join in his self-offering. Christ remains present in the consecrated host even after Mass is over, and we have the opportunity to renew and extend the adoration and communion that occurs during the Eucharistic celebration.

Some parishes have perpetual adoration allowing parishioners the opportunity to adore Jesus twenty-four hours a day, seven days a week. A parishioner can choose to pray with Jesus for an hour or half-hour any day of the week.

We only need to read the Gospel accounts of Jesus' agony in the garden to find where this practice finds its origin.

"Jesus went with his disciples to a place called Gethsemane. When they got there, he told them, 'Sit here while I go over there and pray.'

"Jesus took along Peter and the two brothers, James and John. He was very sad and troubled, and he said to them, 'I am so sad that I feel as if I am dying. Stay here and keep awake with me.' Jesus walked on a little way. Then he knelt with his face to the ground and prayed, 'My Father, if it is possible, don't make me suffer by having me drink from this cup. But do what you want, and not what I want.' He came back and found his disciples sleeping. So he said to Peter, 'Can't any of you stay awake with me for just one hour? Stay awake and pray that you won't be tested. You want to do what is right, but you are weak'" (Matthew 26:36–41).

Don't let the idea of spending an hour keep you from adoration. You can stop by for a short visit or stay as long as you want. The amount of time you spend is up to you. You might be surprised that an hour spent in prayer with Jesus is simply not enough.

"You are my Lord and my God!"
(John 20:28)

Palm Sunday/Holy Week

During the weeks of Lent, we have focused on different aspects of the season. This week we especially focus on Palm Sunday and the sacred Triduum, the three-day period that begins with the Mass of the Lord's Supper on Holy Thursday and ends with the Easter Vigil Mass on Holy Saturday.

Lent leads us to this holiest week of the liturgical year. This week opens with great jubilation on Palm Sunday; it turns solemn with the Mass of the Lord's Supper on Holy Thursday; and it ends with hopeful anticipation.

A variety of activities is provided so you can choose those that best fit your children's needs. Some activities call for quiet reflection and others involve group projects or discussions. Some require advance planning in order to gather supplies for craft projects. You may want to flip to the back of the book to the reproducible pages to see if there are any additional materials you might like to use.

Week-at-a-Glance

Teacher/Parent preparation:

Prior to the prayer service, you will need to assemble a cross from Styrofoam, palm leaves from construction paper and create simple flowers from construction paper (1 per child).

Supplies needed for cross and palm leaves:

Styrofoam cross, about 16" tall

11" x 17" green construction paper (1 per child)

pencils (1 per child)

scissors

tape

Directions:

Have children fold construction paper in half lengthwise and cut out a giant egg-shaped "leaf" from the paper. With paper still folded, cut slits in the "leaf," stopping 1 inch from the fold. Open the "leaf" and tape a pencil inside the fold, letting it extend 3 inches from the bottom of "the leaf" to form the "stem."

Supplies needed for prayer experience:

cross (made of Styrofoam)

palm leaves (1 per child)

red construction paper (with a heart already traced on the paper; 1 per child)

scissors

tape

crayons

strips of paper of various colors (1 per child, and large enough for child to write first name)

Children should proceed to the prayer table, waving palm leaves. There, they will place their palm leaves at the foot of the table.

Have children gather quietly around the prayer table and light the Lenten candle.

Say to the children: The weeks of Lent have led us to the holiest week of the year. Our palm leaves remind us of the wonderful welcome Jesus received when he entered Jerusalem more than 2,000 years ago. The people honored him with shouts of "Hooray! God bless the one who comes in the name of the Lord! (Mark 11:9) But later that week, one of Jesus' own disciples betrayed him. The actions of some of the religious leaders and the Roman authorities led to his death on the cross.

Explain that Jesus' death showed God's love for us. Jesus' arms are outstretched, as if to give us a hug. On the cross, Jesus hugged the whole world. (Have the children cut out the red heart as a symbol of how much Jesus loved us.)

Jesus suffered so that we could live forever with him. This shows how much Jesus loves us. Mention that even if your child was the only one in the world, Jesus would have died for him or her. (Pass out the strips of paper and have each child write his or her name on a strip, and then tape it to the Styrofoam cross.)

End the session with one of these prayers.

Closing Prayer for Younger Children
Jesus, thank you for loving me.
I love you, too.

Closing Prayer for Older Children
Lord Jesus, thank you for loving and forgiving me.
How could I ever thank you enough?
Show me how to live a new life with you.

Sunday Dinner

By Diana Jenkins
Illustrated by Jack Hughes

The first Sunday after Grandma's funeral, I didn't want to get out of bed. Especially when I heard, "Aldo! Time to get ready for church!"

I burrowed under the covers, but I could still hear Mom calling. That's the problem with living in a small apartment. "Aldo! Aldo!"

Next, puny fists pitter-pattered on my door, and my little sister Jaime yelled, "Get up!"

So I dragged myself to church, but I didn't pay much attention to the service. All I could think about was how we wouldn't be going to Grandma's house for Sunday dinner after Mass today. Or ever again.

Grandma was the best cook in the world! Every Sunday, the whole family used to drive to her house (which was in the middle of town for everybody) for a big, delicious feast!

But don't think that I only cared about Grandma because of her cooking!

Grandma was the nicest person you could ever meet. She wasn't afraid to show how much she loved us all. She was always hugging and kissing people. Her cooking was just another way that she showed her love.

After Mass, Mom picked up fried chicken for our Sunday dinner. It didn't taste anything like Grandma's chicken! After we ate, the day dragged by like a lazy snail. It didn't seem like Sunday at all—being at home with just Mom and Jaime.

I sat in front of the television and thought about Sunday afternoons at Grandma's. Our family is a big, noisy bunch of people who are all so different from each other that you can't believe they're in the same family. Somehow, Grandma brought us all together every Sunday. We had so much fun!

Mom came into the living room and said,

The Lent–Easter Book

"It's too nice a day to watch television."

"I don't feel like doing anything else," I muttered.

Mom sat down and took my hand. "It's hard, I know," she said. "I miss her, too."

Mom was trying to make me feel better, but I just wanted to feel how I felt. I pulled my hand away and stared at the television until she left. Then I sat there wondering if our family would be getting together much anymore. Without Grandma and her big house, it didn't seem likely.

I could tell you about the next Sunday and all the ones after that, but each Sunday was as depressing as the one before. I hated going to Mass! It was just this unhappy reminder that it was another Sunday without Grandma and her special Sunday dinner.

One Sunday I played sick, but I couldn't fool Mom!

"Aldo," she said after she'd taken my temperature. "Is this about Grandma?"

"I guess," I said, not sure how to explain. "It just doesn't seem like Sunday without Grandma."

Mom's eyes grew wet. "I know," she said. "It was so wonderful the way she brought us all together, wasn't it?"

"Yeah," I choked out of my tight throat.

"I know you're feeling sad, Aldo, but in hard times we need God more than ever," Mom said. "Please get ready for church."

It sounds terrible, but I zoned out as soon as Mass started that morning. I sat and stood and knelt along with everyone else, but I didn't hear anything that Father McBrearty said. It was like my body was in church, but I was really somewhere in the past.

I was just thinking about how Grandma once showed me how to knead bread dough, when a sharp, little elbow poked into my ribs. I looked down and saw Jaime frowning at me.

"What?" I hissed at her.

"You're not saying anything," she whispered.

Mom was frowning our way, so we both faced front. For a moment, I focused in on the service. I realized that we were already at the Eucharistic Prayer part of the Mass. Father McBrearty was just saying, "May all of us who share in the body and blood of Christ be brought together in unity by the Holy Spirit."

After that, my mind flew off again, but this time I wasn't zoning out. I was thinking about the words I'd just heard.

It was the part about being "brought together" that got me. It sounded so much like what Mom had been saying—and I had been thinking—about Grandma bringing our family together. It was cool that something in the Mass and something in my real life went together like that!

Then I realized something else amazing. Grandma brought our family together with her special meals, and when we "share in the body and blood of Christ" in Holy Communion, that was a meal, too! Just like my mixed-up family, all the different people in my church were coming together—for the most special meal of all!

Then I had another cool idea! The night before Jesus died for us, he brought a group of people together to share a meal. Jesus gave us the Eucharist at the Last Supper!

My head was practically spinning as we lined up for

Communion, but I had a good feeling as I received Jesus in the host. I guess it just meant something so...well, real to me!

On the way home from church, I felt better than I had for a long while. Maybe that's why I was able to come up with a great idea!

"Eating a meal brings people together, doesn't it?" I said to Mom.

"Yes, it does, Aldo," she said.

"And no matter how different they are," I went on, "they become like one family for a while, don't they?"

Mom stopped at a red light and looked straight at me. "Are

you trying to tell me something?"

I decided to come right out with it. "We need to have our big Sunday dinners, Mom," I said. "To bring our family together."

"But Grandma's house is sold, Aldo," said Mom. "And nobody else has a big enough place for the dinners. And we all live so far apart!"

"But can't we figure something out?" I said.

Mom looked out the front window until someone honked at her and she had to drive on. Finally, she glanced at me and said, "Yes, I think we can."

Which we did. Mom found out that we could use the parish hall at Grandma's church, which is right in the middle for everybody. Everyone pitches in, and we have a great Sunday dinner. For a while, we're one family again!

So every Sunday, my church family comes together for the Eucharist (one meal). Then my "real" family shares dinner, which makes a second meal! I think Grandma would be happy to know I'm so well-fed!

Reprinted from My Friend: The Catholic Magazine for Kids, *Pauline Books & Media, 50 Saint Pauls Avenue, Boston, MA 02130.* www.myfriendmagazine.com

Discussion Starters for Grades K–3

Think of special occasions, like birthdays or family reunions, when your family gathers to celebrate and share a meal. What are some of the things you share at these family gatherings? Do relatives hug or shake hands? Do they share conversations? Good news? Do you share some of your favorite foods? Do you pray before the meal?

- We share some of these same things with our "church family" when we gather for Mass. Which ones do we share?

- What gifts did Jesus share with his apostles during the Last Supper? How do we share these same gifts today?

Discussion Starters for Grades 4–8

Teacher/Parent Preparation:

Obtain for each child copies of the Order of the Mass from a missalette and the readings from a Bible.

Think of family reunions or special anniversaries when family and friends gather to celebrate and share a meal. What are some of the things that you share at these gatherings? Greetings? Hugs or handshakes? Good news? Words of praise? Tips or advice? Does your family share traditional foods? Which are your favorites? Does your family share a prayer before the meal? Do they make plans for another reunion?

- How is the celebration of the Eucharist similar to your special family gatherings?

Look through the photocopies of the Order of the Mass together. Identify the parts of the Mass that correspond to what happens at a family gathering (e.g., Gathering Song: arrival of the family members and greetings; Readings: listening to each other's stories and discovering more about each other's lives, desires, meaning, and how that affects the family as a whole; Preparation of the Gifts:

setting the table and prayer before the meal, etc.).

- In the story, Aldo missed his grandma, but he also missed the tradition of gathering for Sunday dinners. Do you think that coming together with the Church family each week is important?

- Aldo also missed Sunday afternoon dinners at his grandma's house because it was there that his grandma showed how much she loved each family member. Do you see that kind of love in your Church family? What would you want to see in your Church family and in worship together?

Read the following passages about the Last Supper Jesus had with his apostles: from the Gospel of John 13:1–15, 14:1–4, 15:9–15; from the Gospel of Luke 22:19–20.

- What are some of the gifts Jesus shared with his apostles at the Last Supper?

- How do we continue to share those same gifts today?

- How can we thank Jesus for his tremendous gift of love?

Clothespin Crucifix

During Holy Week, we focus on remembering Jesus' love for us which he showed in his crucifixion and death. But we also look forward to the Easter celebration of Christ's triumphant victory over death when he rose from the dead. Help your children reflect on Jesus' perfect sacrifice of love by making crucifixes they can hang on a wall at home.

Supplies needed:

clothespins with metal spring
(11 for each child)

8 1/2" x 11" piece of cardboard
(1 per child)

pencil

ruler

scissors

craft glue

5" piece of cord or ribbon (per child)

Optional: modeling clay for corpus
(the kind that dries out or the kind
you bake)

Directions:

1. Have children remove the metal spring from each clothespin. They should have 22 pieces. (You may want to do this beforehand if you are working with younger children.)

2. Place wooden pieces of clothespins flat side down on the cardboard as follows: 9 vertical and 6 horizontal. (See photo.) (Except for the 3 vertical pieces at the bottom, the thin part of all pieces should face the center.)

3. Trace around the cross, and then remove the clothespin pieces. Cut the cross from cardboard.

4. Cut a small square of cardboard about 1 1/4 by 1 1/4 inches and set aside for later use.

5. Lay the clothespin pieces on the cardboard as in step 2, then glue to cardboard cross.

6. Use modeling clay to make the corpus. When clay is dry, it can be glued to the cross. Or take two wooden pieces of clothespins that are similar in color and glue them together, flat sides back to back. Students will need 4 more pieces for the arms and legs. Lay these pieces on the cross, and then glue them into place. (See photo.)

7. To form the loop for hanging, fold a 5-inch piece of cord (or ribbon) and glue to the back of the cross.

8. Glue the 1 1/4 by 1 1/4-inch piece of cardboard over the section of the cord (or ribbon) that has already been glued to the cross.

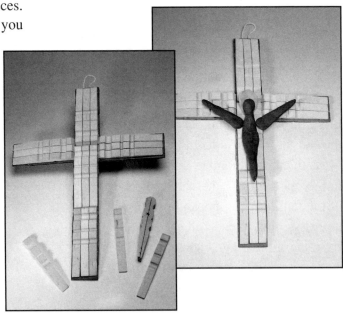

Chalice

Easy

The Mass of the Lord's Supper on Holy Thursday marks the first day of the sacred Triduum. It commemorates the institution of the Eucharist, the institution of the priesthood, and Jesus' command to us to love one another. Help your children to reflect on the Eucharist and the priesthood by making a chalice that can be used as a centerpiece at home throughout the holiest week of the year.

Supplies needed:

- 1 8 oz. Styrofoam or paper cup (for base of chalice)
- 1 12 oz. Styrofoam or paper cup (for cup of chalice)
- 1 sheet aluminum foil, approximately 12" x 17"

rhinestones, beads, or glitter glue

red tissue paper or a piece of red construction paper

wide masking tape

Directions:

1. Wrap both cups in aluminum foil.
2. Roll a piece of masking tape and attach cups, bottom to bottom.
3. Decorate chalice with beads, rhinestones, or glitter glue.
4. Stuff red tissue paper, symbolizing the Precious Blood, into the top cup. You can also cut a circle out of the red paper to fit in the open end of the cup and set it inside.

Reflection

We have a particular penchant for "individual" penances to fill the days of Lent. What about a "family" resolution to turn this Lent into a 40-day track meet for family growth. Some families benefit from deciding to soften the way they speak with each other, offering to help out where needed, praying for each other, communicating more—kids sharing with parents where they've been and what they've been doing, parents expressing to their children the love and acceptance they long for.

Sr. Kathryn James, FSP

Light of Christ Candle

Even the darkness of death could not extinguish the light of Christ. On the third day he rose, conquering sin and death. Help your children understand the significance of the paschal candle by making these candles.

Supplies needed:

12, 16, or 20 oz. plastic beverage bottle (1 per child)

scissors   ribbon

small silk flowers

quick-drying craft glue

8 1/2" x 11" white paper

black, red, and blue markers

yellow or orange paper

Teacher/Parent Preparation:

Cut off the top and bottom of the bottle.

Directions:

1. Tie a ribbon around the neck of the bottle, and then glue on silk flowers.

2. Attach top to the bottom with craft glue.

3. Roll white paper to form the "candle," making sure it fits into "candle holder." Use glue to keep paper from unrolling.

4. Using markers, decorate "candle" as you read the Rite aloud.

5. Place the "candle" into the holder, using craft glue if necessary.

6. Cut a flame from yellow or orange paper and glue it to the top.

7. Drip white craft glue onto candle to form "melting wax."

Rite for Christ Candle

Show children what the candle will look like. Explain that as you pray the "Rite" aloud, they will make the appropriate marks on their candles.

As you pray the prayer, you show actions in parentheses on the board.

$$A$$
$$2 \mid 0$$
$$\overline{0} \mid$$
$$\Omega$$

1. Christ yesterday and today (have children mark the vertical arm of the cross)

2. the beginning and the end (horizontal arm)

3. Alpha (alpha, above the cross)

4. and Omega (omega, below the cross)

5. all time belongs to him (the first numeral [of current year] in upper left corner)

6. and all the ages (second numeral in the upper right corner)

7. to him be glory and power (the third numeral in the lower left corner)

8. through every age for ever (the last numeral in the lower right corner). Amen.

By his glory and glorious wounds may Christ our Lord guard us and keep us.

May the light of Christ, rising in glory, dispel the darkness of our hearts and minds. Amen.

(You may wish to have this last prayer photocopied so the class can pray it together.)

Flower or Butterfly Pens

Butterflies and flowers remind us of new life. Both thrive in the warmth of the sun. We too thrive in the presence of the Son. Jesus Christ is our Lord and God.

Help your children to make these colorful pens to use during the Easter season or to give as Easter gifts, along with the Prayer Journal found on page 21.

Supplies needed:

pens (non-click, non-cap; at least 1 per child)

1 1/2 yards of yarn

foam sheets, various colors (one 8 1/2" by 11" piece yields 3 or 4 "pen toppers"; use scraps for details)

scissors

wiggly eyes

hole punch

fast-drying tacky glue

sequins, beads, glitter

stapler

Directions:

1. Have children tie a piece of yarn to pen, nearest the point, using a double knot. Do not trim off the "tail" of the knot, but hide the "tail" under the yarn as they wrap the entire length of the pen with the rest of the yarn.

2. When pen is completely wrapped with yarn, tie a double knot at the end and trim excess yarn.

3. Choose a design from the templates, or come up with one of your own. Children should trace the design onto foam sheets. They will need 2 of each design, one for the front and one for the back of their pen "toppers."

4. Glue or staple "toppers" together along the sides and top, but not the bottom. Add decorative pieces using more foam, sequins, beads, wiggly eyes, or glitter. (Form tiny circles with foam using the hole punch.)

5. Once "toppers" are dry, glue "toppers" to tops of pens using fast-drying tacky glue.

Reflection

The "sacrifices" we choose for ourselves during the 40 days of Lent remind us that we are good, that we are sacred and saved, that there is more to life than immediately meets our eyes. Giving up a favorite TV show or candy bar creates room for spirit and for the Invisible.

Sr. Kathryn James, FSP

Patterns for Pens

Easter Bible Cookies

This is a special recipe to make with your family on Holy Saturday. It is a prayer experience and a recipe rolled into one! As you complete each step of the recipe, explain to your children how it relates to the passion, death, and resurrection of Jesus. Then have one person read the Scripture passages provided.

Ingredients:

1 cup whole pecans

1 tsp. vinegar

3 egg whites

a pinch of salt

1 cup sugar

Supplies needed:

a zip-lock type baggie

wooden spoon

medium size mixing bowl

waxed paper

cookie sheet

masking tape

Bible

Optional:
In case of allergies, skip the pecans and step 2.

Directions:

1. Preheat oven to 300 degrees.

2. Have children place pecans into zip-lock-type baggie, and then break pecans into small pieces with a wooden spoon. Set nuts aside for later.

Explain to children: This reminds us that Jesus was beaten by the soldiers.

Reader: "Pilate gave orders for Jesus to be beaten with a whip" (John 19:1).

3. Have one child measure 1 teaspoon of vinegar and let everyone smell it before pouring it into the mixing bowl.

Explain to children: This reminds us that when Jesus was dying on the cross he was very thirsty, but they only gave him some cheap wine that tasted like vinegar.

Reader: "Jesus said, 'I am thirsty!' A jar of cheap wine was there. Someone then soaked a sponge with the wine and held it up to Jesus' mouth. After Jesus drank the wine, he said, 'Everything is done!' He bowed his head and died" (John 19:28–30).

4. Have children add egg whites to vinegar.

Explain to children: Eggs represent life, so they remind us that Jesus gave his life for us so that we could have "life to the fullest."

Reader: "I came so that everyone would have life, and have it in its fullest. I am the good shepherd, and the good shepherd gives up his life for his sheep" (John 10:10–11).

5. Sprinkle a tiny bit of salt into each person's hand. Have them taste it then add a pinch of salt to the bowl.

Explain to children: The salt represents salty tears Jesus' followers shed after his death.

Reader: "A large crowd was following Jesus, and in the

crowd a lot of women were crying and weeping for him" (Luke 23:27).

Explain to children: So far, the ingredients don't seem as if they would be tasty. But now we add the cup of sugar. The sweetest part of the story is that Jesus died because he loves us so much!

6. Add sugar, a little at a time.

Reader: "I live by faith in the Son of God, who loved me and gave his life for me" (Galatians 2:20).

7. Now, have children take turns beating the ingredients (except nuts) with a mixer at high speed for about  12 to 15 minutes or until mixture forms stiff peaks.

8. Have children gently mix in broken nuts and then drop the mixture by teaspoons onto a waxed paper covered cookie sheet.

Explain to children: Each mound represents the rocky tomb where Jesus' body was placed.

Reader: "Joseph of Arimathea put the body of Jesus in his own tomb that had been cut into solid rock and had never been used. He rolled a big stone against the entrance to the tomb and went away" (Matthew 27:60).

9. Place the cookie sheet into the oven, close the door, and turn the oven OFF. Seal the oven door with masking tape.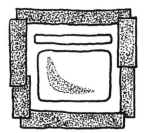

Explain to children: This represents how the tomb was sealed shut.

Reader: "Pilate said to them, 'All right, take some of your soldiers and guard the tomb.' So they sealed it tight and placed soldiers there to guard it" (Matthew 27:65–66).

10. Now, go to bed!

Explain to children: You may be disappointed leaving the cookies in the oven overnight. That's how Jesus' followers felt when he died and was buried.

Reader: "Jesus said, 'I tell you for certain that you will cry and be sad.… But later I will see you, and you will be so happy that no one will be able to change the way you feel'" (John 16:20, 22).

11. On Easter morning, open the oven and give everyone a cookie. Notice the cracked surface and hollow center.

Explain to children: When Jesus' followers came to the tomb, they were amazed to find it empty! Jesus is alive!

Reader: "It was almost daybreak on Sunday when Mary Magdalene and the other Mary went to see the tomb. Suddenly a strong earthquake struck and the Lord's angel came down from heaven. He rolled away the stone and sat on it…. The angel said to the women, 'Don't be afraid! I know you are looking for Jesus, who was nailed to a cross. He isn't here! God has raised him to life, just as Jesus said he would. Come, see the place where his body was lying. Now hurry! Tell his disciples that he has been raised to life and is on his way to Galilee. Go there, and you will see him'" (Matthew 28:1–2, 5–7).

Explain to children: Now it's up to us to share the Good News today!

The Lent–Easter Book

Palm Sunday/Holy Week

Dear Parent(s),

During the Lenten season, we have been focusing on different aspects of Lent: its meaning, its symbols, its customs, and its traditions. The Lenten season comes to a close on the evening of Holy Thursday with the Mass of the Lord's Supper. This week's Take-Home Pages are filled with activities that can help your child better understand the significance of Holy Week. As with the weeks of Lent, these Take-Home Pages are divided into three sections: Warm-Up Exercises, Getting Started, and Putting It into Practice. The theme for this week is Palm Sunday/Holy Week. May the activities suggested in these pages provide you with additional tools for nurturing your child's faith.

Warm-Up Exercises...

Gather the family around your Lenten candle. Add the palm you received at the Palm Sunday Mass to your Lenten symbols on the table. Have one member of the family light the candle and another read the passage from Scripture.

A reading from Mark 11:1–10

Jesus and his disciples reached Bethphage and Bethany near the Mount of Olives. When they were getting close to Jerusalem, Jesus sent two of them on ahead. He told them, "Go into the next village. As soon as you enter it, you will find a young donkey that has never been ridden. Untie the donkey and bring it here. If anyone asks why you are doing that, say, 'The Lord needs it and will soon bring it back.' "

The disciples left and found the donkey tied near a door that faced the street. While they were untying it, some of the people standing there asked, "Why are you untying the donkey?" They told them what Jesus had said, and the people let them take it.

The disciples led the donkey to Jesus. They put some of their clothes on its back, and Jesus got on. Many people spread clothes on the road, while others went to cut branches from the fields.

In front of Jesus and behind him, people went along shouting, "Hooray! God bless the one who comes in the name of the Lord! God bless the coming kingdom of our ancestor David. Hooray for God in heaven above!"

After sharing this passage with your family, follow up with a family discussion using the materials provided.

Explain to your family that palms were used as symbols of victory back in ancient times. When the people greeted Jesus with palms, they showered him with praise and honor. How do we, as a family, honor Jesus today?

How will we, as a family, honor Christ's passion and death this week?

Look over the schedule of liturgies and activities your parish has to offer during Holy Week, especially during the sacred Triduum, the three-day period that begins with the Mass of the Lord's Supper and lasts until the Easter Vigil Mass on Holy Saturday. Decide which liturgies and activities your family will attend. Try to attend as many as possible. If for some reason your family can't attend some of the liturgies, make sure to find time to share the day's readings from Scripture.

Getting Started...

Now have someone read the following passage.

A reading from Mark 14:26–30

During the meal Jesus took some bread in his hands. He blessed the bread and broke it. Then he gave it to his disciples and said, "Take this and eat it. This is my body." Jesus picked up a cup of wine and gave thanks to God. He then gave it to his disciples and said, "Take this and drink it. This is my blood, and with it God makes his agreement with you. It will be poured out, so that many people will have their sins forgiven. From now on I am not going to drink any wine, until I drink new wine with you in my Father's kingdom."

Now have a family discussion about the special gift Jesus shared with his disciples at the Last Supper, the gift of the Eucharist. Jesus shares this gift with us at the Mass.

Jesus is present in the liturgy in the bread and wine that become the Body and Blood of Jesus. What look like bread and wine has truly become Jesus' Body and Blood. When we receive the Eucharist, we become more and more the Body of Christ.

Talk about what could be different in the family if everybody became more and more like Jesus. Write a family prayer everyone can say after they receive Communion.

Putting It into Practice...

If at all possible, plan a special meal for Holy Thursday. Include symbolic foods like lamb, a loaf of bread (unsliced), and grape juice for children, wine for adults. Before sharing the meal, thank God for the gift of his Son and the gift of the Eucharist.

Make sure to explain to your children the significance of the symbolic foods and drinks. The lamb is a symbol for Jesus, the perfect, sacrificial Lamb. The loaf of bread reminds us of the bread Jesus blessed, broke, and shared with his apostles at the Last Supper; it also reminds us that Jesus is the Bread of Life. The grape juice and wine are symbols for Jesus' blood shed for the sins of all people of all times.

After the meal, take part in the celebration of the Mass of the Lord's Supper.

On Good Friday, make a special effort as a family to pray the Stations of the Cross, observe quiet time during the hours between noon to three, read one of the Gospel accounts of Christ's passion, or take part in the Good Friday liturgy.

On Holy Saturday, spend some quiet time reflecting on Jesus' great love for us.

Enlist the help of the entire family to prepare for the coming celebration of Easter by "spring cleaning" the house and replacing Lenten symbols with ones that reflect soon-to-be Easter joy. You might also want to help with the "spring cleaning" at church.

Palm Sunday

Palm Sunday is the first day of Holy Week. It is the day we commemorate Jesus' triumphant entry into Jerusalem. Blessed palms are distributed at all of the Masses. Many families place these palms in prominent places at home, for example, behind a crucifix or a framed picture of Christ. These palms are kept until the following year, when they are returned to church to be burned for ashes that will be used on Ash Wednesday.

Holy Thursday

Many Catholic families begin their observance of the sacred Triduum with the evening Mass of the Lord's Supper.

Others start their observance with a special commemorative meal before the Mass of the Lord's Supper. Symbolic foods are an important part of this meal, including lamb, which represents Jesus, the Lamb of God, who died for our sins; unsliced bread, grape juice (or wine), which symbolize the Eucharist. The bread should be broken and shared; the juice or wine (whichever is appropriate) should be shared by everyone at the table. Additional foods complete the simple, yet symbolic, meal. Then later that evening, the family shares another meal: the Eucharist. When planning your special commemorative meal, remember to plan it early enough in the evening so that your family can receive Communion. As Catholics we do not eat for at least an hour before receiving Jesus in the Eucharist.

Good Friday

For many families, Good Friday is a day of quiet reflection, especially during the hours between noon and three in the afternoon. Televisions and video games are turned off. Radios are silenced. Boisterous activities cease. It is a somber time to reflect on Christ's ultimate sacrifice of love.

Many families take the opportunity to pray the Stations of the Cross at noon. Others choose to attend a later liturgy where the passion of our Lord is read and the cross is venerated. Both services help families reflect on Christ's selfless gift of love.

Holy Saturday

Many families spend the day preparing for Easter. Spring-cleaning is one of the traditional activities for the day. It is a symbolic gesture of preparing one's home for the risen Lord, as we have already prepared our hearts by receiving the sacrament of Reconciliation.

In some parishes, another tradition many families share is the blessing of Easter foods. Families typically take a basketful of food that will be served on Easter to church on Holy Saturday to have it blessed.

Many families also enjoy cooking, coloring, and decorating eggs on Holy Saturday.

If you've never colored eggs using natural ingredients like red and yellow onionskins, coffee, blueberries, beets, cranberries, or red cabbage, you might want try it this year. Simply place 2 tablespoons of vinegar to a quart of boiling water, and then add a handful of natural ingredients. Simmer for about 20 minutes and then sieve the skins or berries from the homemade liquid "dye." Let cool to lukewarm and place hard-boiled eggs into "dye," allowing them to sit for about 5 minutes.

Easter

With the beginning of the Easter season (a season that lasts seven weeks and ends with Pentecost), we will be focusing on the gift of new life in Christ. During the first week of this joyous season, we focus on the celebration of Easter. We also look at Divine Mercy Sunday, the first Sunday following Easter.

If you haven't already replaced the Lenten symbols on your prayer table at school or your dining room table at home, now is the time to do it. Simply remove the purple ribbon from your grapevine wreath, add spring silk flowers to your barren wreath, with butterflies or a bird's nest filled with eggs, and replace the purple candle with a white candle—all symbols of new life.

Week-at-a-Glance

Teacher/Parent preparation:

Replace the Lenten symbols with Easter symbols. See suggestions on page 106.

Supplies needed:

- a basketful of plastic Easter eggs, the kind that open (1 per child)
- small slips of paper
- pencils or pens
- Handel's "Hallelujah Chorus" on CD or another appropriate song
- CD player

Gather the children around the prayer table and light the Easter candle. Say to the children: During Lent our prayer table held Lenten symbols. Today it holds symbols of the Easter season, symbols of new life. Throughout the seven-week season of Easter, we sing or say "alleluia" throughout the celebration of Mass. Alleluia is an expression for glory and praise. In Hebrew, it means "Glory to him who is." During today's prayer experience, we will be writing our own words of glory and praise.

Directions:

While passing out plastic eggs and slips of paper to each of the children, explain that they are to write a simple prayer of praise, then place that prayer inside the egg, and place the egg back into the basket. Allow time for the children to write their prayers. Once all the children have placed their eggs in the basket, put the basket on the prayer table. Tell the children you will be sharing one of these prayers each day. Have one child open an egg and read to the class the "prayer of praise" found inside.

Next, explain that Handel's "Hallelujah Chorus" is a song of praise, a "prayer"

through song. Have them close their eyes to help them focus on the "Hallelujah Chorus" as a prayer.

Play the CD.

Afterward, end with one of these prayers.

Closing Prayer for Younger Children:
Jesus is risen! Alleluia! Alleluia!
Let us be glad! Amen! Alleluia!

Closing Prayer for Older Children:
Jesus is risen! Alleluia! Alleluia!
He is Lord forever and always. Amen! Alleluia!

Remember: Each day an egg will be opened and a child will read the "prayer of praise." This can be done with morning prayers, Grace before meals, or with bedtime prayers at home.

Reflections

The One who was crucified and rose again is the Lord of the world and of history. Easter casts its light on the whole cosmos and illumines it. It is the light of love and truth which redeems the universe from death caused by sin, and renews the plan of the creation, so that all things may acquire their full meaning and be reconciled with God and with one another.

John Paul II

———

Today is the day of the resurrection: May all people rejoice and say:
"Friends and enemies alike—we forgive everything today!"
Christ is risen! He is truly risen!

Orthodox Liturgy

Is Jesus Alive?

If so, where is he?

By Sandra Humphrey and illustrated by Virginia Esquinaldo

Jamal tapped on his glass with a knife and called for attention. "Okay, guys, let's get started. If we're ever going to get this essay done, we've got to focus."

Allison shoveled a piece of pizza onto her plate and picked up her pen. "Okay, tell us again what we have to do and I'll jot down our ideas."

Jamal wiped imaginary sweat from his forehead and frowned. "What we have to do is explain why we do or do not believe in the resurrection and, if we do believe in the resurrection, how we know that Jesus is still a real part of our lives today."

Krista picked the mushrooms off her pizza and shrugged. "The first part is easy. I think we all believe in the resurrection. That's what Christianity is all about—how Jesus voluntarily died on the cross for all of us and then rose from the dead."

Emilio helped himself to a large slab of pizza. "But that second part is pretty hard. How do we know that Jesus is still real in our lives today when we can't even see him or talk to him?"

Allison squeezed her eyes shut, something she always did when she was thinking. "I think it's all a matter of faith. Remember our youth group last Wednesday night when Father Hardy gave each one of us a puzzle piece and asked us to describe the puzzle? Well, of course, no one could because we each just had one small piece and that doesn't tell you much about the whole puzzle."

Jamal stopped inhaling his pizza and nodded his head. "And then we broke up into our small discussion groups. We talked about living each day by faith. With just our one puzzle piece, we don't know what the puzzle is eventually going to look like. But we know that Jesus can see the whole puzzle because he always sees the larger picture instead of just the little bit that we see."

Then Emilio broke in. "In our small group I talked about the time when I was almost five and I wanted this cheap, little toy car so badly. I just about had a temper tantrum right there in the store, but my Dad wouldn't get it for me. And then I found out later that he was getting me a really cool red tricycle for my birthday the next week and that's why he didn't get me the cheapie toy I wanted. I think Jesus looks after us the same way. He can always see the big picture, and we just have to trust him."

Emilio scrunched up his forehead and shook his head. "But how about when really bad things happen? Like when the Nelsons' home burned down last month and they lost everything in the fire?"

Allison nodded. "That was bad news. But how about the good news? Nobody died in the fire, and everyone pitched in to help them. People who didn't even know them helped clean up the mess, and hundreds of people donated stuff."

"And how about all those people who offered to share their homes with the Nelsons until they could find somewhere else to live?" Jamal added. "It seems like sometimes bad times bring out the best in people. It's what I like to call, 'bringing out the Jesus' in people."

Emilio broke into a huge grin. "Hey, man, I really like that. I think you're right. I think hard times can 'bring out the Jesus' in people."

Allison began waving her pizza crust in the air. "Hey, I just thought of something! Doesn't it say somewhere in the Gospels, 'Where two or three are gathered in my name, I am there with them'? So Jesus is alive and present

wherever Christians come together."

Krista stopped in the middle of pouring herself a glass of milk. "Of course—why didn't we think of that before! Remember Mrs. Pilon's last quiz—the four ways Jesus is present in the celebration of the Eucharist."

Emilio ticked them off on his fingers. "In the people who've come together for Mass; in the priest who represents Christ; in the Scripture readings; and especially in the bread and wine, which have become the Body and Blood of Christ."

Jamal grinned. "I think we're on to something. The Eucharist and the other sacraments—didn't Jesus give

them to the Church as a way to stay with us even after he rose and ascended into heaven?"

"Yeah, the Church and sacraments," chimed in Allison. "That's how we get the grace that helps us to live as Jesus did and…."

"…do good for others, like people did for the Nelsons!" finished Emilio.

Jamal pointed to the assignment sheet in front of him. "I think we got it! What do you say?"

Everyone nodded and Emilio slapped Jamal a high-five.

"Got it!" said Allison scribbling away. "'We think Jesus is most definitely alive, really alive!' How's that as the opening sentence of our essay?"

Reprinted from My Friend: The Catholic Magazine for Kids, *Pauline Books & Media, 50 Saint Pauls Avenue, Boston, MA 02130.* www.myfriendmagazine.com

Easter Renewal of Baptismal Promises

Supplies needed:

large bowl
holy water (you can get this at church)
paper towels

Teacher/Parent preparation:

Place the bowl on a table and pour in some holy water.

At Easter, we renew the promises that we made at Baptism, the first sacrament we received that made us members of the Church. Does anyone have pictures of their own Baptism? Has anyone been present at a Baptism? What are some of the things that you remember from the Baptism?

After Jesus rose from the dead, he appeared to his apostles and then returned to his Father in heaven. Jesus dwells on earth in his Church, and through the sacraments he gives us life and salvation.

Most of us received Baptism as infants. We were not able to say our baptismal promises for ourselves—our godparents answered the questions for us. Do you know who your godparents are?

Invite the children to gather around the bowl filled with water. Tell them that they will now be renewing their baptismal promises by responding, "I do" to the series of questions you ask.

Leader: Do you reject Satan and all his works and all his empty promises?

All: I do.

Leader: Do you believe in God the Father almighty, creator of heaven and earth?

All: I do.

Leader: Do you believe in Jesus Christ, his only Son, our Lord, who was born of the virgin Mary, was crucified, died, and was buried, rose from the dead, and is now seated at the right hand of the Father?

All: I do.

Leader: Do you believe in the Holy Spirit, the Lord, the giver of life, who proceeds from the Father and Son?

All: I do.

Leader: Do you believe in the holy Catholic Church, the communion of saints, the forgiveness of sins, the resurrection of the body, and life everlasting?

All: I do.

Invite each of the children to approach the bowl of holy water, dip the fingers of their right hand into the water, and make the Sign of the Cross.

At the end of the ceremony you can pray together the *Our Father.*

Discussion Starters for Grades K–3

- In the story you just heard, Jamal, Emilio, and Allison named four ways that Jesus is with us during the Eucharist. Can you name them?

- How is Jesus present in our classroom at school? With your family at home? In your neighborhood?

- How can you bring the love of Jesus to others?

Reflection

The One who was crucified and rose again is the Lord of the world and of history. Easter casts its light on the whole cosmos and illumines it. It is the light of love and truth which redeems the universe from death caused by sin, and renews the plan of the creation, so that all things may acquire their full meaning and be reconciled with God and with one another.

John Paul II

Discussion Starters for Grades 4–8

- If someone asked if you believe in the resurrection, what would you tell him/her? What reasons would you give to support your belief?

- Emilio, Jamal, and Allison mentioned four ways that Jesus is present in the Eucharist. Can you name them?

- How is Jesus present in your life today? In your classroom at school? In your family? In your neighborhood? In the lives of the poor and suffering? In areas of the world where wars rage?

- How do you help others to see the presence of Jesus in their lives?

Have the children use their Bibles to find passages from Scripture that hold eyewitness accounts of Christ after his resurrection. Try Matthew 28, Mark 16, Luke 24, and John 20 and 21.

Compare the readings from the different Gospels.

- How are they similar? Do they share the same basic story?

- Why do you think Jesus appeared to his disciples after his death?

- How often do you read the Bible?

- How does the Bible help us to grow in faith?

- Name other ways that can help you grow in faith.

- How can you find more time to share with Jesus?

- How can you share your faith with others?

- How can you encourage your friends to want to know Jesus?

- How can you encourage your friends to grow in faith?

Reflection

There is no body! Now the Body of Christ, crucified and risen from the dead, lives in the world. Resurrection is hard to believe in, let alone explain. We need a community to help us with words, with remembering, and with holding onto hope in the face of death.

Megan McKenna

Easter Tree

Easy

Eggs remind us of new life. In the spring we see birds' nests filled with eggs. Before long, tiny birds peck their way out of darkness and into the light of the world. Christ, too, emerged from darkness to light on Easter morning. Help your students/children understand that an egg can remind us of the tomb that surrounded Jesus in darkness until he rose on Easter morning.

Supplies needed:

2–3 dozen colored plastic Easter eggs

a roll of thin string

Easter stickers

fabric paintbrush or a small tree limb with branches

scissors

ruler

clear tape

Directions:

1. Have the children decorate the eggs. Encourage them to be creative and make each egg look special.

2. Measure and cut the string into different lengths so that the eggs will hang at different levels on the "tree" branches.

3. Attach a piece of string to each egg. Open the egg by gently twisting and pulling the two halves apart. Then, fasten the string to the inside of the egg with a small piece of tape. (See the illustration.) Put the two halves of the egg back together and close them as tight as you can. (The string should be thin enough so that the egg can still fasten and stay closed.)

4. The children can take turns "hanging" the eggs on the tree. They may need someone to "help" them tie the string and to make sure that the eggs get evenly spaced apart.

After all the eggs are hung on the "tree," invite the children to gather around it, join hands and sing a well-known Easter song, like "Jesus Christ Is Risen Today."

Seeded Eggs

Easy

Help your children recognize eggs and seeds as symbols for the new life at Easter by making these unique egg decorations for a seaonal table centerpiece.

Supplies needed:

Styrofoam eggs (at least 1 per child)

a variety of seeds (either birdseed or plant seeds will do)

craft glue

decoupage

sponge brushes

craft sticks

waxed paper

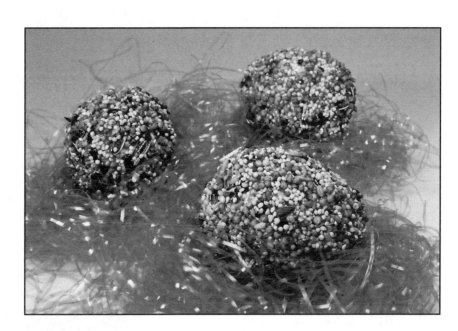

Directions:

1. Lay a sheet of waxed paper on work surfaces. (Children will place their eggs on the waxed paper to dry.)

2. Pour seeds into a large bowl or container.

3. Spread craft glue over entire Styrofoam egg, using a craft stick to spread the glue.

4. Roll glue-covered egg in seeds, making sure seeds cover the entire surface of egg. Add seeds where needed. Children should press seeds firmly onto the egg, and then place the egg on waxed paper to dry.

5. Once glue has dried and seeds are secured, brush decoupage over the entire egg and again place on waxed paper to dry.

6. Make a variety of eggs with different types of seeds. These eggs can be placed in a bowl or basket with Easter grass as a decoration at home.

Reflections

Come, then, all you nations, receive forgiveness for your sins. I am your forgiveness. I am the Passover that brings salvation. I am the lamb who was immolated for you. I am your ransom, your life, your resurrection, your light; I am your salvation and your king.

St. Melito of Sardis

———

When Christ says: "Do not be afraid," he wants to respond to the deepest source of the human being's existential fear. He means do not fear evil, since in his resurrection good has shown itself stronger than evil. His Gospel is victorious truth.

John Paul II

Chicks: New Life

Easy

Baby chicks are symbols for new life. Chicks emerge from the darkness of their shells into the light of life outside. Help your children understand the meaning of this symbol while creating cute little chicks from pompoms and paper.

Supplies needed:

1 large yellow pompom or 2 beige or
  yellow pompoms (per child)

2 wiggly eyes (per child)

orange card stock

scissors

clear-drying craft glue

yellow thread

templates for the feet and beak

Directions:

1. Cut the beak and feet from orange card stock.

2. Glue 2 large pompoms together, or have children tie yellow thread around the large pompom to divide it into the head and body. (See photo.)

3. Glue on the eyes, feet, and beak.

4. Cut a circle from orange card stock and glue it onto the bottom so that the chick won't "roll away."

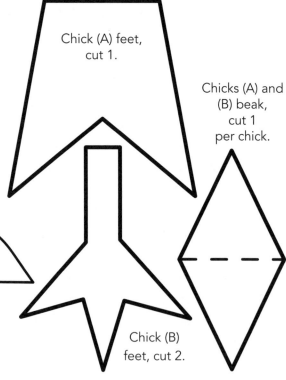

Chick (A) feet, cut 1.

Chicks (A) and (B) beak, cut 1 per chick.

Chick (B) feet, cut 2.

Chick (A) crest, cut 1. Fold on dashed line.

Chick (B) crest, cut 1. Cut slits on dashed lines (for "feathers").

The Lent–Easter Book

Easter Lily

The flower most associated with Easter is the lily, fragrant and white. Its striking trumpet-like shape announces that Easter is here!

Supplies needed:

white foam sheet or card stock (4 1/2" x 4 1/2" square per flower)

scissors

craft scissors with patterned edges (optional)

bamboo skewer

wrapped candy or yellow ribbon (for the inside of the lily)

craft glue

green ribbon (12" per flower)

Directions:

1. Have children cut a 4 1/2 by 4 1/2 inch square from foam sheet or card stock.

2. Cut off 1 of the corners so that the diagonal cut measures 1 inch.*

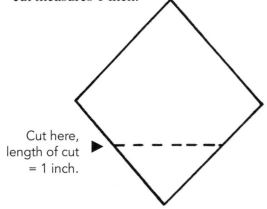

Cut here, length of cut = 1 inch.

3. Place the square of foam sheet or card stock on the table with cut corner at the bottom. Glue the bamboo stick to the square.

4. Fold in 2 corners to form a cone, then glue to hold.

_____

* Note that the "cut corner" measures one inch.

5. Place candy inside flower and secure with a dab of glue.

6. Tie a green ribbon around the bamboo, form a bow, and glue the bow in place.

Reflection

Faith is the only possibility we have of entering into contact with Christ. "Who believes in Christ," says St. Augustine, "touches Christ." By faith, St. Paul says, Christ dwells in our hearts (cf. Eph. 3:17).

Raniero Cantalamessa

Easter Bookmarks

Easy

Encourage your children to spend time reading and studying Scripture, and help them mark their favorite passages with these colorful Easter bookmarks.

Supplies needed:

foam sheets of different colors

large paper clips of different colors

tacky craft glue

scissors

pencils

Optional: permanent markers

Templates (bottom right column):

heart (Divine Mercy)

sheep (Good Shepherd)

flame (Pentecost)

candle (faith)

cross (resurrection)

Directions:

1. Have children trace the templates to use as patterns for bookmarks.

2. Trace the patterns for the bookmarks onto foam sheets and cut them out. Cut 2 of each shape.

3. Glue 1 shape to the upper end of a paper clip, and then glue the other shape on top of the paper clip to form a "sandwich."

4. Children can add decorative details using permanent markers.

Plant an Indoor Garden

Gardening is a wonderful activity that teaches lessons about nurturing life. Comparisons can be made between planting seeds in the garden and planting "seeds of faith." Both need nourishment; both need constant care. As plants grow and mature, they stretch for the sun. As we grow in faith, we grow closer to God the Father, the Son, and the Holy Spirit. As plants need nourishment from the soil to flourish, we need nourishment from God through Scripture, the sacraments, and prayer.

Depending on where you live, it may be too early to start an outdoor garden, but it's not too early to start one inside. By starting now, your seedlings should be ready to transplant about the time of Pentecost. So jump right in. Plant some seeds, and nourish the "seeds of faith" you've already planted!

Tips for planting an indoor garden:

Choose easy to grow herbs such as mint, chives, basil, thyme, or cilantro; easy-to-grow veggies such as lettuce, beans, peas, carrots, cucumbers, zucchini, or pumpkins; or easy to grow flowers such as sunflowers, zinnias, or marigolds.

For herbs, fill 6-inch clay pots with potting soil. Plant the seeds according to the directions on the seed packets. For veggies and flowers, fill 3-inch peat pots with potting soil and plant seeds.

Place pots in a sunny location—a window facing south or west—where the plants will get five or more hours of sunlight every day.

Keep the soil moist until the seeds sprout, and then follow directions for care found on seed packets. Make sure to place pots on trays to catch any excess water.

As soon as all danger of frost is gone, transplant your seedlings, peat pot and all, to a suitable location in your garden. Herbs can be kept in pots and placed outside until late fall, when they can be brought back inside.

Establish a routine for watering, weeding, and feeding. Then enjoy the fruits of your labors.

"The seeds that fell on good ground are the people who hear and welcome the message. They produce thirty or sixty or even a hundred times as much as was planted" (Mark 4:20).

The Easter Vigil

Since the earliest years of the Church, Holy Saturday has been held as a vigil for Jesus, our Savior and Lord. So it's not surprising that many Catholic families begin their Easter celebration with the vigil Mass on Holy Saturday. For adults and older children who have participated in the RCIA or RCIC program, and for their families and friends, the Easter Vigil is especially meaningful. This is when the candidates, or "elect," are welcomed into the Church with the sacraments of initiation: Baptism, Confirmation, and the Eucharist. The vigil begins in a darkened church, which gradually moves to light, beginning with the lighting of the paschal candle. The liturgy of the Word, which can include up to nine separate readings, follows this ceremony of light. The readings focus on the great things God has done throughout salvation history. Then the candidates are "born again" through Baptism; they are welcomed into the Church. The vigil proceeds with the celebration of the Eucharist. This year ask your pastor or parish council to consider having a reception to welcome the new members.

The Alleluias Are Back!

Many parishes and parish day schools "bury" the alleluias before Lent begins in a special ceremony with music and song. Often an "alleluia" banner is carried in procession to the front of the church where it is displayed throughout the Mass or prayer service. Numerous alleluias are said or sung throughout the Mass or service, then the banner is carried out during the recessional song, "buried" in a box, or placed in a dark closet or cupboard until it is "resurrected" at Easter. Then it is displayed in church and accompanied with the numerous alleluias, which are prayed or sung throughout the Easter season. Some families hold their own special ceremonies at home, followed by hanging the "alleluia" banner outside for the rest of the Easter season.

Easter Clothes

For years, Easter outfits included new shoes, dresses, hats, and purses; new shirts, ties, and slacks. Though today's "Sunday's best" isn't nearly as formal, many families still celebrate Easter by wearing new clothes. This practice is symbolic; it recognizes our new life in Christ. It is based on biblical references. If your family enjoys this Easter tradition, be sure to explain to your children the reason for wearing new clothes.

"All of you are God's children because of your faith in Christ Jesus. And when you were baptized, it was as though you had put on Christ in the same way you put on new clothes" (Galatians 3:26–27).

Easter Baskets

Surely, one of the most popular customs we share on Easter Sunday is the giving of Easter baskets. Typically, these baskets are filled with candies in shapes symbolic of the season: crosses, eggs, bunnies, and chicks. For those who prefer to give baskets without sugary treats, here are a few ideas.

An Easter basket for the little gardener: Fill the basket with quick-growing flower and vegetable seeds, peat pots, garden gloves, and little gardening tools. These items will pro-

The Lent–Easter Book

vide hours of fun indoors and out, and will provide "seeds" for discussion. Parents should explain that just as seeds spring into life when planted and cared for, so does our faith in Jesus.

An Easter basket for the budding bird-watcher: Fill the basket with a bird-watching book, seed, suet, and a bird feeder or house. Share with children the gift of nature, and remind them that just as we care for and feed the birds, Jesus cares for us and feeds us with the Bread of Life.

An Easter basket for kids who love good news: This basket holds an age-appropriate Bible, CD or cassette of Christian music, and Bible-based puzzles and games. Remind your children that Jesus came to share the Good News. We need to share the Good News with others, too.

Easter Eggs

Pysanky are traditional Ukrainian Easter eggs, known for their beautiful, intricate designs. For decorative purposes, true *pysanky* are made with raw eggs. In this simplified version, the eggs are cooked. Though time-consuming to create, they're absolutely beautiful. Placed in a basket with Easter grass, they make an attractive, edible centerpiece.

Supplies needed:

hard-boiled eggs
pastel-colored egg dyes
candle
pencils with erasers
sewing pins
blow dryer
paper towels

Directions:

1. Dye hard-boiled eggs.
2. Make your "egg-decorating tool" by pushing a pin into the pencil eraser.
3. Light candle and dip tip of "tool" into melted wax and apply the wax to an egg that has already been dyed a pastel color, using designs symbolic of this holy season.
4. Once the wax sets, dip the egg into a darker color. Wherever you applied the wax, the color will remain the same. Remove egg from the dye, and blot dry with paper towel.
5. Apply another design with wax. Dip egg into a different color. Repeat this process several times until you have the design you desire.
6. Once finished with design, use blow dryer to melt the wax, and then wipe with a paper towel.

The New and Improved Easter Egg Hunt

Hunting for Easter eggs is a tradition many families hold. The custom can have great spiritual meaning. You will need about a half dozen plastic eggs (the kind that open) per child. Inside each egg, hide a clue that directs your child to the next egg; each egg brings him/her closer to the egg with the "prize." The "prize" could be an age-appropriate Bible, a book about the saints, a copy of *My Friend* magazine with a subscription, or other resources to nourish their growing faith. Once your child finds the prize, you can explain that just as the "clues" led them to their "prize," God's Word leads us to the "prize" of eternal life.

Easter and Divine Mercy

Dear Parent(s),

Now that we are into the Easter season—a season that lasts seven weeks—we will be focusing on the gift of new life in Christ.

We replace the Lenten symbols with symbols of new life by replacing the nails with butterflies, a bird's nest with eggs or some silk spring flowers, and replacing the purple candle with a white candle.

These Family Take-Home Pages are filled with activities to reinforce what we're learning and discussing in class. They are divided into three sections: Warm-Up Exercises, Getting Started, and Putting It into Practice. The themes for this week are Easter and Divine Mercy.

May the activities suggested in these pages provide you with additional tools for nurturing your child's faith.

Warm-Up Exercises...

Gather the family around the white candle. Have one member of the family light the candle, and another read this passage from Scripture.

A reading from Matthew 28:5–8

The angel said to the women, "Don't be afraid! I know you are looking for Jesus, who was nailed to a cross. He isn't here! God has raised him to life, just as Jesus said he would. Come, see the place where his body was lying. Now hurry! Tell his disciples that he has been raised to life and is on his way to Galilee. Go there, and you will see him. That is what I came to tell you." The women were frightened and yet very happy, as they hurried from the tomb and ran to tell his disciples.

After sharing this passage with your family, follow with a family discussion using the suggested questions.

What did the women find when they visited the tomb? What did the angel tell them to do? And what was their response? What is OUR response to the good news of Jesus' resurrection? How are we sharing this "wonderful news" with others? What else can we do to share the news?

Getting Started...

Brainstorm with your family different ways that you can celebrate Easter. Here are a few ideas to get you started:

Plant a tree or sapling as a symbol of your family's growing faith. Have everyone help with the digging and planting, watering and mulching. Bless it with a prayer.

Make an Easter banner to hang out or indoors. Display it throughout the Easter season.

Make a commitment to grow in faith by joining a Bible study or other group at your parish.

Putting It into Practice...

Establish a new Easter custom with your family by celebrating Divine Mercy Sunday, the second Sunday of Easter. When canonizing St. Faustina in 2000, Pope John Paul II declared this day Divine Mercy Sunday, because the revelations of Jesus to St. Faustina so powerfully express the central truths at the heart of the Gospel: the merciful love of God manifest especially in the passion and resurrection of his Son.

Bake and decorate a heart-shaped cake. You can pray the Divine Mercy Chaplet before eating the cake.

The **Divine Mercy Chaplet** is prayed on rosary beads.

1. Begin by praying one Our Father, one Hail Mary, and one Apostles' Creed.

2. Then on the Our Father beads say:

   Eternal Father, I offer You the Body and Blood, Soul and Divinity of Your dearly beloved Son, Our Lord Jesus Christ, in atonement for our sins and those of the whole world.

3. On the Hail Mary beads say:

   For the sake of His sorrowful Passion, have mercy on us and on the whole world.

4. At the end, pray three times:

   Holy God, Holy Mighty One, Holy Immortal One, have mercy on us and on the whole world.

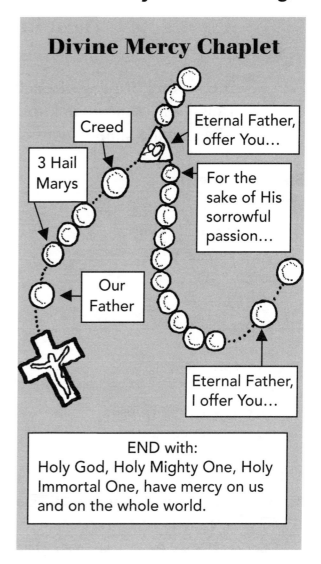

Divine Mercy Chaplet

Creed

3 Hail Marys

Eternal Father, I offer You...

For the sake of His sorrowful passion...

Our Father

Eternal Father, I offer You...

END with:
Holy God, Holy Mighty One, Holy Immortal One, have mercy on us and on the whole world.

Find out more about Divine Mercy Sunday on the web at: www.marian.org

Reflection

Know, My daughter, that between Me and you there is a bottomless abyss, an abyss which separates the Creator from the creature. But this abyss is filled with My mercy. I raise you up to Myself, not that I have need of you, but it is solely out of mercy that I granted you the grace of union with Myself.

Tell souls not to place within their own hearts obstacles to My mercy, which so greatly wants to act within them. My mercy works in all those hearts which open their doors to it. Both the sinner and the righteous person have need of My mercy. Conversion, as well as perseverance, is a grace of My mercy.

Message of Jesus to St. Faustina

Trust in My Pocket

The second Sunday of Easter is known as Divine Mercy Sunday. Help your children acknowledge Jesus' love and mercy for us with these heart-shaped cards.

Supplies needed:

heart template (see page 123)

red construction paper

white computer paper

scissors

pencil

hole punch

magic markers
   or colored pencils

small stamps
   or cards depicting Jesus

string for hanging

Directions:

1. Have children trace the heart template onto red construction paper, then cut out.

2. Once again, trace the template onto white computer paper, only this time trim the heart so that it will be a bit smaller than the first heart.

3. On white heart, write "Jesus, I trust you," and decorate.

4. Fold each heart as indicated on the template.

5. Open the heart. Using glue stick, glue the white heart inside the red heart.

6. Punch a small hole at the top of the heart, thread a string through the hole, and tie it to form a loop for hanging.

7. On the outside of the card write "Jesus loves me" or glue on a picture of Jesus.

Reflections

Come… I will bring you to the heights of heaven. With my own right hand I will raise you up, and I will show you the eternal Father.

St. Melito of Sardis

———————

Don't run. Don't hide. Don't blend back into the world!
We must give an account of our hope!

Megan McKenna

Heart Template

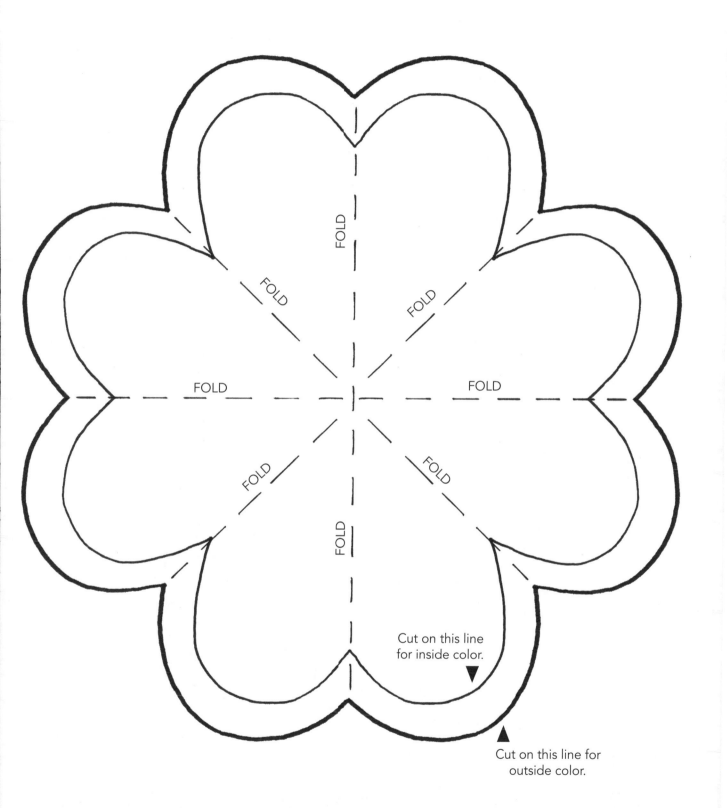

FOLD

FOLD

FOLD

FOLD

FOLD

FOLD

FOLD

FOLD

Cut on this line
for inside color.

▼

▲

Cut on this line for
outside color.

Jesus Is My Shepherd

The Church celebrates Good Shepherd Sunday on the fourth Sunday of Easter. At the Eucharistic liturgy on this day, we hear the story of Jesus, the Good Shepherd, who is willing to give up his life for his sheep. "I am the good shepherd. I know my sheep, and they know me. Just as the Father knows me, I know the Father, and I give up my life for my sheep" (John 10:14).*

Supplies needed:

colored card stock or construction paper (1 sheet per child)

pencils

scissors

ruler

ribbon

sheep template (page 125)

small white pompoms or cotton balls

wiggly eyes (2 for each sheep)

white poster board

Directions:

1. Have children cut a 5 by 10 inch rectangle.

2. Trace a 3 1/2 inch circle in the upper half of the rectangle. Then have them cut out the circle.

3. Glue a ribbon from the top of the circle to the bottom of the back of the rectangle.

4. Cut a sheep from the white poster board, using the template provided on page 125.

5. Glue white pompoms or cotton balls to the body of the sheep, and then have children glue 2 wiggly eyes to the face of the sheep.

6. Finally, glue the sheep to the ribbon. Before gluing, place another piece of paper under the ribbon to absorb the excess glue.

7. After the glue dries, write across the bottom: *Jesus is my Shepherd*, or, *I'm safe with Jesus.*

back side of the card

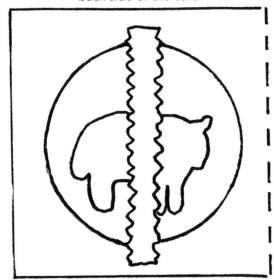

* Before making this craft, you may want to read aloud the entire story of the Good Shepherd, found in the tenth chapter of John's Gospel.

Jesus Is My Shepherd Card template (page 124)

Shepherd's Staff bookmark
template (page 127)

FOLD

▲

Cut out this circle from
the front of the card.

Use this as a pattern for
the lamb.

▲

You
Lord,
are
my
shepherd.

I
will
never
be
in
need.

Psalm 23:1

Sheep Magnet template
(page 126)

Sheep Magnets

Easy

The image of Jesus as the Good Shepherd is very comforting to those who are troubled or burdened with cares. You can make this craft and give it to someone who needs a little encouragement, or to a newly baptized member of the Church. With their magnetic backs, they hang easily on refrigerator doors where you'll be sure to see them.

Supplies needed:

8 1/2" x 11" white and tan craft foam sheets (each sheet yields 4 sheep)

black construction paper (1/2 sheet per child)

white construction paper (1/2 sheet per child)

(Alternative: cotton balls)

scissors

fast-drying craft glue

permanent markers

wiggly eyes, 1 per sheep

clothespins, the pinch style (1 per child)

magnetic strips, self-stick, 3" per sheep

templates (see page 125)

Directions:

1. Have children trace templates (page 125) for "body" and for "fleece" onto foam sheets, then cut out.

2. Glue "fleece" to "body" and "eye" to "face" of sheep. Alternative: Glue cotton balls on the sheep's body instead of white "fleece."

3. Add details to "face" and "fleece" with permanent markers. (See photo.)

4. Glue sheep to clothespin.

5. While waiting for glue to dry, write notes of encouragement on card stock. (See photo.)

6. Once glue is dry, apply sticky-back magnetic strips to clothespins, then clip note to clothespin and give as a gift to someone special.

"The sheep know their shepherd's voice. He calls each of them by name and leads them…" (John 10:3).

The sheep know their shepherd's voice. He calls each of them by name and leads them…
John 10:3

Shepherd's Staff Bookmark

Easy

The image of the Good Shepherd is a comforting one for children as well as adults. Help your children to mark the pages of their reading materials with bookmarks that remind them of the Good Shepherd who leads us "home."

Teacher/Parent Preparation:

Fabric should be prepared ahead of time. To do this, you will need to fuse the fabric together using Wonder Under and a hot iron. Follow the manufacturer's directions. This will make the fabric stiff and keep it from fraying. When the fabric is cool to the touch, cut fabric into 30 rectangles, measuring 3 by 7 inches.

Supplies needed:

- template (See page 125.)
- 1 yard of 45"-wide tan cotton fabric (yields 30 bookmarks)
- 2 yards of Wonder Under or other fabric stiffener (it comes in a standard width of 18")
- iron
- 10 yards of ribbon, 1/4" wide (enough for 30 bookmarks)
- fabric markers
- pinking shears
- hole punch

Directions:

1. Have children trace the template for the shepherd's staff onto their rectangle of prepared fabric.

2. Cut out the "staff" using pinking sheers.

3. With fabric markers, copy this verse (or another) from the Bible onto the bookmark:

"You, Lord, are my shepherd. I will never be in need." Psalm 23:1

4. Punch a hole in the top of the "staff" using the hole punch.

5. Fold a piece of ribbon 12 inches long and slip the folded end through the hole, then slip the loose ends of the ribbon through the fold and pull the loose ends to form knot.

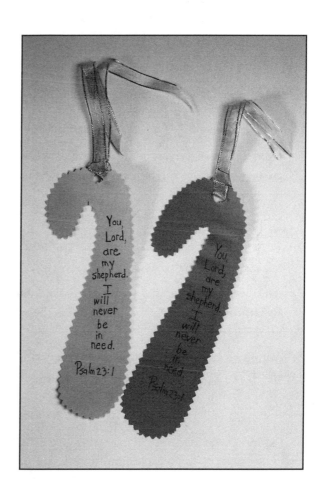

Jesus Is the Gate

Jesus is the Way, the Truth, and the Life. He is also the Good Shepherd and the gate leading us to eternal life. These gate-like plaques with Bible verse can be hung by magnetic strips or by ribbons.

Supplies needed:

craft sticks, 15 regular (or 11 wide) per child

fast-drying craft glue

white acrylic paint*

brushes (foam brushes work best)

markers

1 1/2" x 2 1/2" rectangle cut from construction paper (1 per child)

pens

heart-shaped buttons, beads, wooden or foam cut-outs (1 per child)

string or yarn

paint shirts or smocks

newspaper

Directions:

1. Have children spread newspaper over work surfaces and put on their paint shirts.

2. Paint 15 regular size or 11 wide craft sticks white.

3. Form an outline of a square using 4 craft sticks, and glue ends where they overlap.

4. Lay 11 regular size or 7 wide craft sticks on top of the "square outline," then glue these sticks in place.

5. While glue is drying, copy this verse from the Bible onto the 1 1/2 by 2 1/2 inch rectangle of construction paper: "I am the gate. All who come in through me will be saved." John 10:9

6. Cut a 3-inch length of yarn. Glue the ends of the yarn to the 2 top corners of the paper to form "sign" on "gate."

7. Glue the corners of the rectangle to the "gate."

8. Next, glue ONLY the midpoint of the yarn to the "gate," then glue heart on top of yarn. (See photo.)

9. When glue dries, add final details (handle and hinges) to "gate" with markers.

10. Tie a ribbon to the plaque, or attach self-stick magnetic strips to the back of plaque for hanging.

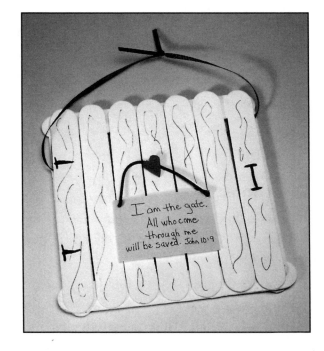

---

* Whenever working with paints, have children spread newspaper on work surfaces and wear paint shirts, smocks, or other protective clothing.

Baking Bread

You will want to bake this bread ahead of time since it takes a few hours. While you share this delicious loaf of bread with your children, also share the story of the Last Supper. Explain how Jesus instituted the sacrament of the Eucharist so that he could be with his followers even after he died and ascended into heaven. Jesus, our Savior and Lord, is also called the Bread of Life.

Ingredients:

- 2 pkgs. fast-acting dry yeast
- 2 cups warm water
- 1 tbs. salt
- 1/2 cup sugar
- 1/8 tsp. ginger
- 1/4 cup vegetable oil
- 2 eggs
- 6–6 1/2 cups flour
- butter (to melt over the crust when removed from the oven)

Directions:

1. Dissolve yeast in warm water according to the directions on the package.

2. Stir in sugar, salt, ginger, oil, and eggs. Mix well.

3. Then add 3 cups of flour and beat until smooth. Continue adding flour until dough is easy to handle.

4. Turn dough onto a floured board and knead until smooth and elastic, about 5 minutes.

5. Place dough into a large greased bowl and cover with towel. Let rise in a warm place until it doubles in size, or about 1 hour.

6. Punch down dough. Divide dough in half and roll each half into a rectangle 9 by 18 inches.

7. Roll up dough and place seam down in a greased 9 by 5 by 3 inch loaf pan. Cover with a towel and let rise until double, about an hour.

8. Then bake at 375 degrees for 30–35 minutes or until golden brown. Melt butter on crust to keep crust soft.

9. Remove loaves from pans and place on wire racks to cool. Let cool before slicing.

When Jesus Knocks Doorknob Hangers

Easy

Help your children to express their faith with these easy-to-make door-knob hangers.

Supplies needed:

pre-cut doorknob hangers (available in craft stores) or foam sheets to cut out your own

regular scissors

craft scissors for cutting patterned edges

clear-drying craft glue

paints* or markers (markers dry faster)

Directions:

1. Have children spread newspaper over work surfaces and put on their paint shirts.

2. If they need to cut the doorknob hangers shape from foam sheets, you can use the template on the right.

3. Use craft scissors with patterned edges to trim the edges of foam sheets.

4. Print this or some other proclamation of faith on the sheet using paints or markers: "I open when Jesus knocks." Optional: have children come up with their own personal proclamation about Jesus.

5. Add decorative touches using clear-drying glue, yarn, cord, sequins, beads, and scraps of foam.

---

* Whenever working with paints, have children spread newspaper on work surfaces and wear paint shirts, smocks, or other protective clothing.

Cut on solid line. ▶

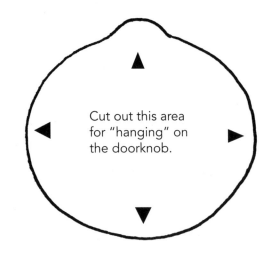

Cut out this area for "hanging" on the doorknob.

"Knock and it will be opened to you," says Jesus.

Matthew 7:7

Window Greetings

Easy

Help your children to share the Good News with super-simple window greetings.

Use a bar of soap, window markers, or foam sheets. Note: Foam sheets provide the perfect material for window greetings. Simply wet the foam letter and apply to the glass. No tape. No paints. No mess.

Supplies needed:

8 1/2" x 11" foam sheets (allow 1 sheet per letter; the number of sheets needed will depend on the length of the message)

scissors

craft scissors with patterned edges

paper (for making block letter patterns)

pencils

Directions:

1. Have children vote on a greeting that they'd like to display on their windows. Select one from those suggested or come up with one of your own. Count the number of letters needed for their greeting, and then determine who will make each letter.

2. Before cutting out letters, make sure children sketch them onto paper first. Then use the paper letters for patterns. Make the letters large enough so the greeting can be read from a distance.

3. Optional: They may want to cut out the letters using craft scissors with patterned edges.

Suggestions for window greetings:

I am with you always.

We believe!

Amen! Alleluia!

Praise God!

Jesus lives!

Jesus is real life.

I'm never alone.

Believe in Jesus.

Peace be with you.

Jesus, now and forever.

"…Why are you men from Galilee standing here and looking up into the sky? Jesus has been taken to heaven. But he will come back in the same way that you have seen him go" (Acts 1:11).

Ascension

Dear Parent(s),

During the Easter season—a season that lasts seven weeks—we have been focusing on the gift of new life in Christ. This week we focus on the Ascension.

This Take-Home Page is filled with activities to reinforce what we're learning and discussing in class. It is divided into three sections: Warm-Up Exercises, Getting Started, and Putting It into Practice. May the activities suggested here provide you with additional tools for nurturing your child's faith.

Warm-Up Exercises...

Gather the family around the Easter candle. Have one member of the family light the candle, and another read this passage from Scripture.

A reading from Luke 24:46–51

He told them: "The Scriptures say that the Messiah must suffer, then three days later he will rise from death…. So beginning in Jerusalem, you must tell everything that has happened. I will send you the one my Father has promised, but you must stay in the city until you are given power from heaven."

Jesus led his disciples out to Bethany, where he raised his hands and blessed them. As he was doing this, he left and was taken up to heaven.

After sharing the reading from Scripture, discuss how your family shares the Good News with others.

Getting Started...

Before Jesus ascended to heaven, he shared a final blessing or prayer with his followers. Ask your family: How often do we, as followers of Jesus, pray? How often do we share blessings and prayers with others? Starting today, make an effort to spend more time in family prayer.

Here are a few suggestions to get you started: Extend your meal-time prayer by having your family pray for the intentions of others, especially for those who don't have anyone to pray for them. Establish a daily family "prayer time" when everyone in the family prays for and with each other.

Putting It into Practice...

Now is a perfect time to help your family learn to appreciate the Catholic tradition of the novena, which dates back to the time of the apostles. Novena means "nine." A novena is any prayer that is prayed for nine days in a row. Why nine days? Because we know that during the nine days between Jesus' Ascension (40 days after Easter) and Pentecost (50 days after Easter), the disciples met in prayer as they waited for the Holy Spirit to come. "The apostles often met together and prayed with a single purpose in mind" (Acts 1:14).

Holy Spirit Ornament

"Suddenly there was a noise from heaven like the sound of a mighty wind! It filled the house where they were meeting. Then they saw what looked like fiery tongues moving in all directions, and a tongue came and settled on each person there" (Acts 2:2–4).

The Holy Spirit is sometimes described as wind and fire, sometimes as a dove. Make these symbols of the Holy Spirit, and then hang them in the classroom or at home.

Supplies needed:

white computer paper
yellow computer paper
template
2 wiggly eyes per ornament
black magic marker
scissors
pencil
craft scissors with patterned edges
white thread
white glue or glue stick

Directions:

1. Have children cut the dove template out of yellow paper. They will also cut a slit on the body of the dove where indicated.

2. Using craft scissors with patterned edges, cut the yellow paper into a rectangle 6 inches by 5 inches, then fold it accordion style into 5 even folds. (See diagram below.)

3. Repeat step 2 using white paper. Both the white and yellow papers will be used as "wings."

4. Insert both folded "wings" into the slit.

5. Glue the edges of the yellow and white papers together to extend the wing span above the dove. (See diagram below.)

6. Insert thread through a small hole in the top of the wings, to form a loop for hanging the dove. Glue on wiggly eyes.

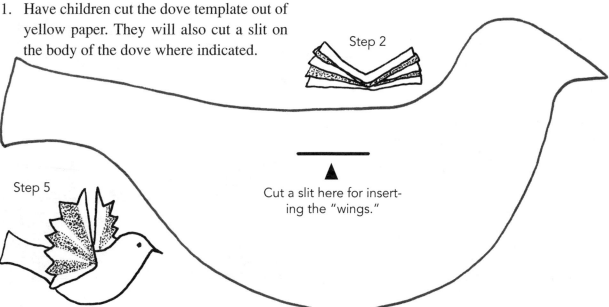

Step 2

Step 5

Cut a slit here for inserting the "wings."

Sachets

When Jesus ascended into heaven, God sent the Holy Spirit to remain with Jesus' disciples. Though the disciples saw the Spirit for only a short time on Pentecost, they knew that the Spirit remained with them. This craft demonstrates to young children that just because we can't see something doesn't mean it isn't there. The sachet is hidden in a drawer, but its scent is a reminder that it is near. This craft helps children to understand that though they can't see the Holy Spirit, they can experience his presence in other ways.

Supplies needed:

scented soap, 1 per sachet

tulle, 12" circle per sachet (circles of tulle sold in packages of 10 or more)

glitter paint

small silk flowers, a few per sachet

ribbon, 12" of ribbon per sachet

Directions:

1. Have children paint a fragrant bar of soap with glitter paint and let dry.

2. Place soap in center of a piece of tulle, gather with ribbon, and secure with a knot.

3. Place a few silk flowers on the ribbon, tie another knot around the stems, and form a bow.

Optional:

Have older children break the soap into several chunks before painting with glitter paint.

"Then the eleven disciples went to Galilee, to the mountain where Jesus had told them to go. When they saw him, they worshiped him; but some doubted. Then Jesus came to them and said, 'All authority in heaven and on earth has been given to me. Therefore, go and make disciples of all nations, baptizing them in the name of the Father and of the Son and of the Holy Spirit, and teaching them to obey everything I have commanded you. And surely I am with you always, to the very end of the age'" (Matthew 28:16–20).

A Special Thank You

The Spirit blesses everyone with different gifts. In turn, we share our gifts with others. Help your children to recognize their gifts, and the gifts that others share with them. Then have the children express appreciation by making these "gifts" to share with others.

Supplies needed:

2 1/2" x 3 1/2" foam sheet rectangles (1 per child)
> Note: One 8 1/2" x 11" foam sheet yields 6 rectangles

3" x 5" card stock (or index card) (1 per child)

scissors

ribbon, 6" per gift box

sequins, glitter, beads

fast-drying craft glue

permanent markers

clothespins, the pinch style (1 per child)

magnetic strips, self-stick, 3" per clothespin

Directions:

1. Using the foam rectangle as the "gift box" have children decorate it on one side with sequins, glitter, or beads.

2. Tie a ribbon into a bow, then glue the bow onto the foam gift box.

3. Glue the gift box onto a clothespin.

4. While waiting for the glue to dry, write thank you notes on card stock. (See photos on right.)

5. Once the glue is dry, apply sticky-back magnetic strips to clothespins, and then clip the thank you card to the clothespin.

Reflection

Christ's resurrection has opened a way to God for the world.

Hans Urs von Balthasar

Pentecost

Dear Parent(s),

During the Easter season—a season that lasts seven weeks—we have been focusing on the gift of life in Christ. This week we focus on Pentecost.

This Take-Home Page is filled with activities to reinforce what we're learning and discussing in class. It is divided into three sections: Warm-Up Exercises, Getting Started, and Putting It into Practice. May the activities suggested here provide you with additional tools for nurturing your child's faith.

Warm-Up Exercises...

Gather the family around the Easter candle. Have one family member light the candle, and another read this passage from Scripture.

A reading from Acts 2:1–4

On the day of Pentecost all the Lord's followers were together in one place. Suddenly there was a noise from heaven like the sound of a mighty wind! It filled the house where they were meeting. Then they saw what looked like fiery tongues moving in all directions, and a tongue came and settled on each person there. The Holy Spirit took control of everyone, and they began speaking whatever languages the Spirit let them speak.

After sharing the Scripture reading, discuss how the Spirit was present with Jesus' disciples on the first Pentecost, and how the Spirit is present in your lives today.

Getting Started...

Again, have one family member read this short passage from Scripture.

"There are different kinds of spiritual gifts, but they all come from the same Spirit. There are different ways to serve the same Lord, and we can each do different things. Yet the same God works in all of us and helps us in everything we do" (1 Corinthians 12:4–6).

Now ask your family to consider the different "gifts" the Spirit has given to each member. Have everyone take turns looking into a hand-held mirror, while other family members suggest the "gifts" they see in the person looking in the mirror. When everyone has had a turn, thank them for sharing their gifts with each other. Thank God, too, for blessing each of you with these gifts.

Putting It into Practice...

Red is the color for Pentecost. It reminds us of the fiery tongues that descended on Jesus' disciples. Celebrate Pentecost by setting a festive table for dinner; include a bouquet of red flowers and place a small box, gift-wrapped with red tissue paper, in the center of the table to symbolize the "gifts" the Spirit has given each of you.

Have family members decide how they can share their gifts, and start doing so this week!

Reproducible Pages

Reproducible Pages-at-a-Glance

The Sacrament of Forgiveness and Peace

By Sr. Maria Grace Dateno, FSP

Have you ever tried to run a race or play a soccer game while carrying your backpack full of school books? That would be pretty hard, wouldn't it? You wouldn't be able to do your best because of the weight of the backpack. The weight would really slow you down.

Did you know there are other "bags" we carry that slow us down on our journey to our Heavenly Father? These are not bags of books, but they are things that make it hard for us to follow in the footsteps of Jesus. If you could look into your "bag," you might see the time you lied to your parents; or when you made a face at your sister out of jealousy; or the time you cheated on a test; or when your mom had to drag you to Mass on a Sunday. You would see all the things you had done that were wrong and all the good things you had neglected to do, that you should have done. These are sins.

Probably none of these sins would be mortal sins (seriously wrong things that completely break off our friendship with God). But all these smaller sins are a burden we carry that slows us down. They tire us out. They prevent us from running freely in the footsteps of Jesus.

Everybody carries around these kinds of bags, everyone in your family, in your school, and in your parish. Sin makes it hard for all of us to live as the family of God.

Jesus knows how hard it is to carry around the weight of our sins. So he gave us a special gift to help us get rid of these burdens and really feel free. There is a special sacrament in which we can experience God's forgiveness in a wonderful way. This sacrament has several names. It is called the sacrament of Reconciliation, the sacrament of Penance, confession, and the sacrament of forgiveness.

You can make this little booklet to help you prepare to celebrate this sacrament. You might also like to share the booklet with someone else.

You will need scissors and a stapler. Read the following directions carefully.

1. Cut out the 4 sets of pages on the dotted lines.

2. Lay the pages down with the number tabs all facing up and the tab marked "1" on the top of the pile.

3. Fold the pages in half down the middle so that the cover is on top.

4. Staple your mini-book in the middle and trim off the tabs.

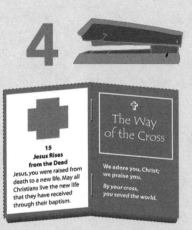

The Lent–Easter Book

1

Thank you, Jesus, for the gift of this sacrament. I am so happy to know that you have forgiven me. Help me to try harder to love you as you love me. Help me to love others as you want me to. Amen.

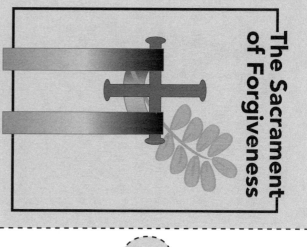

The Sacrament of Forgiveness

Then Father says, "Give thanks to the Lord for he is good." You respond, **"His mercy endures forever."** Father then invites you to go in peace.

Before receiving this sacrament, we ask the Holy Spirit to help us call to mind the wrong things we have done, or the good things we should have done but didn't. We tell Jesus we are sorry for these things. Here are some questions to help you make this examination of conscience.

3

Father then holds his hands over your head and says the words that tell us that God has forgiven us:

who have authority over me?

☐ Was I kind and helpful to my brothers and sisters, friends and neighbors (even those I don't like very much)?

☐ Did I hurt anyone by my words or actions?

☐ Did I make fun of others or exclude them?

☐ Have I lied or stolen?

Then Father will invite you to say an act of contrition (a prayer that says you are sorry for your sins). You can pray this one or any one you know:

When you are ready, go into the reconciliation room or the confessional. After you sit down or kneel down, the priest will greet you. Father says, **"In the name of the Father, and of the Son, and of the Holy Spirit."** You make the sign of the cross and answer: Amen. (Sometimes at this point the priest may read a short reading from the Bible.)

Do your penance as soon as possible afterward, so that you do not forget. The penance we are given helps us to make up for what we have done wrong. It also helps us to change our life and become more like Jesus.

My God, I am sorry for my sins with all my heart. In choosing to do wrong and failing to do good, I have sinned against you whom I should love above all things. I firmly intend, with your help, to do penance, to sin no more, and to avoid whatever leads me to sin. Our Savior Jesus Christ suffered and died for us. In his name, my God, have mercy.

When we turn away from God, like the lamb who strayed from the flock, Jesus, the Good Shepherd, comes looking for us. Jesus has given us a special sacrament to reconcile us with himself through the Church. To be reconciled means to become friends again.

- ☐ Have I been jealous of what others have?
- ☐ Have I treated my body and everyone else's with respect?
- ☐ Have I avoided drugs and anything else that would harm me?
- ☐ Is my language clean?
- ☐ Am I grateful for all I have, including the talents God has given me?

God, the Father of mercies, through the death and resurrection of his Son has reconciled the world to himself and sent the Holy Spirit among us for the forgiveness of sins; through the ministry of the Church may God give you pardon and peace, and I absolve you from your sins in the name of the Father, and of the Son, and of the Holy Spirit.
You answer: **Amen.**

- ☐ Did I make anything more important to me than God?
- ☐ Did I use the name of God and of Jesus respectfully?
- ☐ Did I go to Mass every Sunday and try hard to pay attention?
- ☐ Have I prayed every day?
- ☐ Did I respect and obey my parents and those

Father will listen to you and might ask you questions. He might also give you some advice to help you avoid these sins in the future.

Then Father will give you a penance. It could be prayers to say or good deeds to do.

Now is the time that you tell your sins to the priest. You should also let him know how long it has been since you last celebrated the sacrament.

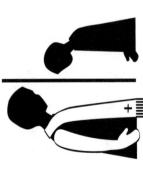

Name _____

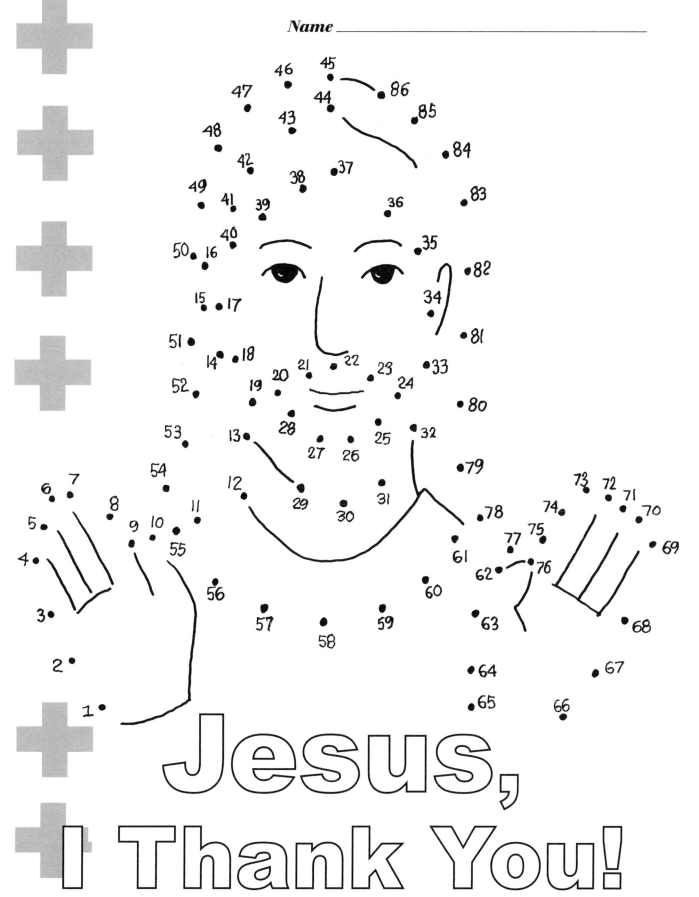

Jesus,
I Thank You!

Name _____

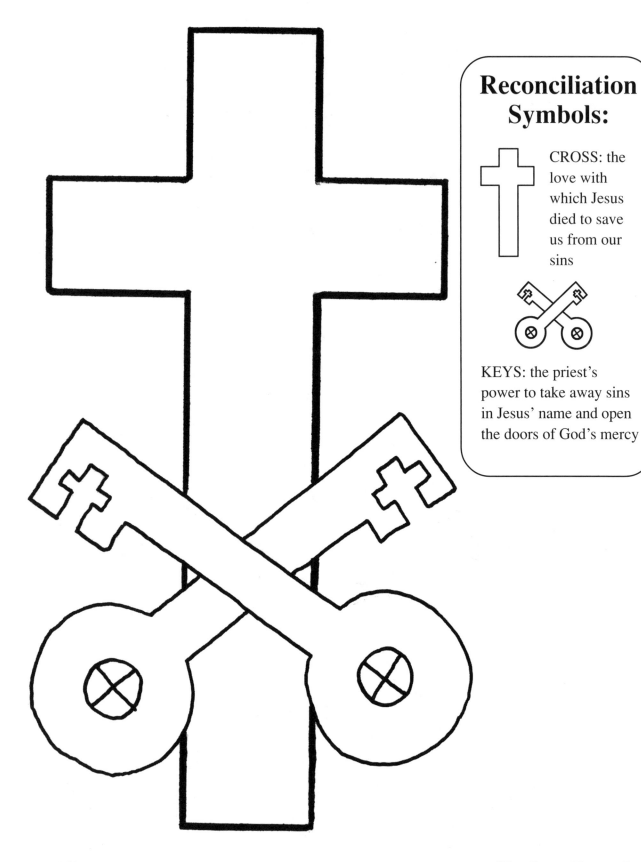

Reconciliation Symbols:

CROSS: the love with which Jesus died to save us from our sins

KEYS: the priest's power to take away sins in Jesus' name and open the doors of God's mercy

Way of the Cross Play

The Way of the Cross centers on fifteen events in Jesus' passion, death, and resurrection. These plays do not present the traditional fourteen stations (see Way of the Cross prayer book on pages 161–170), but, following the example of John Paul II, highlight events specially chosen for use with children.

Though the tone of the plays is simple and conversational, the amount of material to memorize makes them appropriate for middle grade and older children.

Each station, a play in itself, is complete with stage directions and lines. Be sure to allow sufficient time for children to learn their lines, for gathering needed props, and for constructing the crosses.

Props needed for each station:

Station 1: No props required

Station 2: swords, clubs

Station 3: firewood

Station 4: bowl of water, towel, folded piece of paper

Stations 5, 6, 7, 8, 10: cross, grapevine wreath for crown of thorns

Station 9: cross, grapevine wreath for crown of thorns, fabric for veil

Station 11: three crosses, grapevine wreath for crown of thorns

Station 12: three crosses, grapevine wreath for crown of thorns, clothes, cloak, dice

Station 13: three crosses, grapevine wreath for crown of thorns, jar of wine, sponge, stick, sword

Stations 14 and 15: cloth, pottery for holding spices

How to Make Super-Simple Props

The crown of thorns is simply a grapevine wreath, formed to fit the actor's head.

The crosses carried in these plays can be made from heavy-duty cardboard tubes used for upholstery fabrics. Most store managers will gladly donate these tubes, but ask them in advance so that they can set these aside as they are emptied. For younger children, two tubes bound together with masking tape will make a manageable cross to carry. For older children, you may want to use six tubes—three tubes bound together for the vertical "beam," and three for the horizontal "beam." Three crosses are needed, one for Jesus, and one each for the two criminals. So when contacting fabric stores, ask for a total of either six or eighteen.

To form the cross, flatten the mid-section of the two rolls that will form the intersection of the vertical and horizontal pieces of the cross. This will make it easier to bind the rolls together. The rolls for the horizontal bar of the cross will need to be trimmed. After you have crushed and trimmed the rolls, bind the three shorter rolls together at either end with packaging tape; bind the three longer rolls together at either end with packaging tape. Then form a cross with the two bundles and tape them together where they overlap, using plenty of packaging tape.

Rather than making bases in which to stand the crosses hold the crosses in place behind the actors.

The First Station

Jesus in the Garden of Gethsemane

(Characters: Jesus, apostles, Narrator.)

(Curtains open.)

(Right stage: Jesus walking with apostles; Narrator left of stage.)

Narrator: Jesus and his apostles visit one of their favorite places, the garden of Gethsemane. They have just shared the Passover meal. Jesus told them one of them will betray him. All of the apostles are with Jesus in the garden, except for Judas. Knowing what is about to happen, Jesus says to his apostles:

Jesus: Please sit here, while I go over there to pray.

(Jesus motions to the left of stage; apostles sit.)

Apostles: Yes, Jesus. Of course.

Jesus: Peter, James, and John, come with me. My heart is breaking. I feel so sad. Please stay with me and pray.

(Jesus clutches hands to heart. Peter, James, and John follow Jesus, left of stage.)

Peter: Of course, we'll stay with you.

James and *John:* And we'll pray.

Narrator: Jesus' apostles pray in silence. But soon, exhausted from their sorrow, they fall asleep. Still, Jesus continues to pray.

(Jesus kneels, head bowed, lips moving; Peter, James, and John sit and pray, then fall asleep; others lie asleep.)

Jesus: (looking up) Not my will, Father, but yours.

Narrator: Jesus returns to Peter, James, and John. He finds them asleep.

(Jesus taps Peter's shoulder; Peter is startled; Peter nudges James and John.)

Jesus: I know you want to do as I have asked, but you are weak. Stay awake and pray so that you will not enter into temptation.

Narrator: Jesus goes off again, to pray in private.

(Jesus kneels; lips move as if praying; apostles close their eyes.)

Jesus: Father, please help me to do your will.

Narrator: Jesus returns to his apostles. Once again, he finds them asleep and awakens them.

(Jesus walks over and shakes Peter; Peter opens his eyes, wakes James and John.)

Jesus: Can't you stay awake for one hour to pray? Please, do this for me!

Peter: I'm sorry, Jesus.

James and *John:* We're sorry, too.

(Peter, James, John begin to pray.)

Narrator: Again, Jesus goes off to pray in private. He says the same prayer.

Jesus: Not my will, but yours.

Narrator: He returns to his apostles and finds them asleep a third time. But he doesn't get angry. He simply awakens them and says:

(Jesus returns to apostles; wakes them; apostles look embarrassed.)

Jesus: The one who is about to betray me is already here. Come!

(Curtains close.)

Narrator: Sometimes we disappoint our loved ones. Sometimes our loved ones let us down, too. But Jesus, our Savior, will never let us down. Thank you, Jesus, for loving us so.

The Second Station

Jesus Is Betrayed by Judas

(Characters: Jesus, apostles, armed men, Judas, Narrator.)

(Curtains open.)

(Jesus with apostles center stage; Judas, armed men enter stage right.)

Narrator: Judas arrives with a group of armed men. Judas walks right up to Jesus and says:

(Jesus looks sadly at Judas while the apostles and armed men watch.)

Judas: Teacher!

Narrator: Jesus replies:

Jesus: Are you going to betray me with a kiss?

(Judas looks surprised and kisses Jesus' cheek.)

Narrator: When the apostles hear this, they ask Jesus if they should fight. But Jesus replies:

Jesus: Put away your swords! Don't you know that I could ask my Father to send twelve armies of angels to rescue me? He who lives by the sword will die by the sword.

(Jesus turns toward the armed men.)

Jesus: Tell me, why do you come with swords and clubs as if I were a criminal? You've heard me speak in the temple and never arrested me there. Yet, you come to arrest me in the darkness of night!

(Armed men grab Jesus by the arms; apostles huddle together.)

Jesus: If I am the one you want, then let the others go.

Narrator: At once, Jesus' disciples desert him.

(Apostles exit stage, left and right. Then Jesus looks at Judas, but Judas turns away.)

Narrator: Judas remembers what Jesus said at the Passover meal.

(Jesus faces audience to deliver his line.)

Jesus: One of you will betray me.

Narrator: And Judas cringes when he recalls what he said to Jesus.

(Judas cringes, then faces audience.)

Judas: Surely, Teacher, you don't mean me.

Narrator: Suddenly Judas realizes the terrible mistake he has made and he cries out:

Judas: Oh, Jesus, what have I done?

(Judas runs away; exits stage left.)

Narrator: The other men mock Judas.

Armed men (in a mocking tone): Oh, Jesus, what have I done?

Narrator: The men tie Jesus' hands and take him away.

(Jesus led off stage to right; Peter enters stage left.)

Narrator: Peter watches from a distance, and he recalls the time Jesus asked his disciples, "Who do you say that I am?" Peter shudders when he recalls his response:

(Peter faces audience to deliver lines.)

Peter: You are the Messiah sent from God!

(Peter shakes his head, buries his face in his hands.)

Peter: Oh, Jesus, how could we abandon you now?

(He then exits stage left. Curtains close.)

Narrator: Sometimes we run from difficult situations. Sometimes we run from the truth out of fear. Dear Jesus, help us to remember that with you by our side, there is no need to fear.

The Third Station

Peter Denies Jesus

(Characters: Peter, the crowd, woman #1, woman #2, bystander, Narrator.)

(Curtains open.)

(Center stage: small crowd around fire; Peter joins them; Narrator left of stage.)

Narrator: Jesus has been arrested and taken to the house of Caiaphas, the high priest. Peter follows at a safe distance. He sits by the fire in the courtyard. Soon a woman in the courtyard recognizes him.

(Woman #1 stares at Peter, then points.)

Woman #1: You, too, were with Jesus.

(Peter looks surprised and scared.)

Peter: Oh, no! I'm sorry but you are mistaken. I don't know the man!

Narrator: A short time later, someone else says:

(Woman #2 studies Peter, nods.)

Woman #2: I think this man was with Jesus!

Narrator: Again Peter denies it.

(Peter vigorously shakes head; frowns.)

Peter: Oh, no, I wasn't!

Narrator: Feeling uncomfortable and scared, Peter leaves the campfire to stand by himself. An hour passes. Someone else recognizes him.

(Bystander walks by Peter, then does a double take and announces to the crowd.)

Bystander: This man must have been with Jesus. They both come from Galilee.

(Peter glares at bystander.)

Peter: I don't know what you are talking about!

Narrator: But even as Peter is speaking, a rooster begins to crow.

(Sound effect: rooster crowing.)

Narrator: Suddenly Peter remembers what Jesus had said.

(Peter turns to the audience to deliver lines.)

Peter: "Before the rooster crows tomorrow morning, you will deny me three times."

Narrator: Upset that he has denied Jesus, Peter runs from the courtyard and cries.

(Peter runs off stage, exits right.)

(Curtains close; everyone exits stage to left.)

(Curtains open. Peter stands alone, center stage.)

Peter: How could I deny you? You are the Son of God and my friend! Forgive me, Jesus, I pray!

(Peter shakes his head and buries his face in his hands.)

Narrator: Peter also recalls the time Jesus took him to the mountain, along with James and John. There they heard a loud voice come down from a cloud. It said, "This is my dear Son. I am pleased with him. Listen to what he says!"

(Peter shakes his head.)

Peter: Oh, God, how could I deny knowing Jesus? Oh, God! I'm so sorry!

(Peter runs from stage; exits left.)

(Curtains close.)

Narrator: Just like Peter, we can pretend we don't know Jesus, that we are not Christians, that we have never heard about how Jesus asks us to live if we wish to follow him. Jesus, help us, like Peter, discover your forgiveness and mercy.

The Fourth Station

Jesus Is Condemned to Death

(Characters: Jesus, Pilate, two guards, the crowd, Person #1, Person #2, Person #3, Person #4, two soldiers, Herod, Narrator, Messenger.)

(Curtains open.)

(Center Stage: Jesus stands before Pilate, hands tied, silent, guards on either side. Crowd across rear of stage. Pilate studies Jesus.)

(Person #1 points at Jesus.)

Person #1: This man tried to start a riot!

Person #2 (smirking): He claims to be our King!

(Pilate nods.)

Pilate: Is this true? Do you claim to be king?

Jesus (calmly): Those are your words.

(Pilate shrugs, then turns to crowd.)

Pilate: I don't find him guilty of anything.

(The crowd looks shocked.)

Person #3 (yells with hands on hips): But he's been causing trouble all over Judea!

Person #4 (shaking a finger at Jesus): He started in Galilee. Now look where he is!

(Pilate raises his eyebrows. He looks from the crowd to Jesus, then back to the crowd.)

Pilate: So…he's from Galilee?

Crowd (nodding): Yes! He's a Galilean.

Pilate (nodding): Then he shall go before Herod, who is the ruler of Judea.

(Pilate exits stage left. Herod and two soldiers enter stage right. Guards lead Jesus to Herod.)

Narrator: Pilate sends Jesus to Herod. Herod asks Jesus questions, but Jesus doesn't respond.

(Herod gestures as if he's talking with Jesus; Jesus stands silent and still.)

Narrator: Tired of receiving no answers, Herod and his soldiers make fun of Jesus and then send him back to Pilate.

(Soldiers bow to Jesus, laugh, then lead him to Pilate, stage left.)

(Pilate enters stage left. Crowd mumbles among themselves. Herod exits stage right.)

Narrator: Because it is a custom for the governor to release a prisoner during Passover, Pilate wants to release Jesus. But the crowd wants him to release Barabbas, a criminal and convicted murderer. Pilate's wife sends him a message.

(Messenger enters stage left, delivers a note, exits stage left; Pilate reads note.)

Narrator: The note says: "Do not have anything to do with this innocent man. I have had nightmares because of him."

(Pilate tosses the note to the ground and looks from Jesus to the crowd.)

Pilate: He has done nothing to deserve death.

Narrator: But the crowd does not accept Pilate's answer.

(Crowd shakes fists at Pilate and yells.)

Crowd: "We want Barabbas!"

Narrator: Afraid of a riot, Pilate replies:

Pilate: Take Barabbas, but I wash my hands of this. I will not be guilty of this man's death!

(Messenger enters left with bowl of water and towel. Pilate washes and dries his hands.)

(Curtains close.)

Narrator: Dear God, give us the courage to do what is right, even when we must do it standing alone.

The Fifth Station

Jesus Takes Up His Cross

(Characters: Jesus, soldiers, Person #1, Person #2, Person #3, Person #4, the crowd, Narrator.)

(Curtains open.)

(Crowd stretches across stage. Some look sad, some smirk, others pray. Right of stage, Jesus carries cross; two soldiers follow; Narrator is left of stage.)

Narrator: So many people have gathered to watch Jesus carry his cross. The place is buzzing with conversation. People who have heard Jesus preach during the past three years recall some of the things he said.

(Jesus moves slowly across the stage as actors say their lines.)

(Person #1 steps forward to deliver lines.)

Person #1: I heard him preach the Sermon on the Mount. He said, "God blesses those people who are treated badly for doing what is right. They are the ones who belong to the Kingdom of heaven."

(Person #1 bows head in prayer.)

Person #1: Oh, dear God, bless Jesus now. He doesn't deserve any of this!

(Person #1 steps back into the crowd.)

(Person #2 steps forward to speak.)

Person #2: I was there too. I heard him speak. He said, "God will bless you when people insult you and mistreat you, and tell all kinds of evil lies about you because of me." Now the Teacher himself is being insulted and mistreated.

(Person #2 shakes head and steps back into the crowd.)

Narrator: But there are others in the crowd who are happy to see Jesus sentenced to death. And they aren't afraid to speak up!

(Person #3 steps forward, smiling.)

Person #3: It serves him right. He's been stirring up trouble. I can't believe some of the things he's said!

(Person #3 glares over at Jesus, then steps back into the crowd.)

(Person #4 steps forward to speak, then steps back into the crowd.)

Person #4: That's right! Oh, preacher, look at you now!

Narrator: Also among the crowd are those who love Jesus: his mother Mary, her friends, and the apostle John. Their hearts ache for him. They know he doesn't deserve this.

(Mary holds her hands to her heart; Jesus looks sadly at Mary, John, and the women; they look mournfully at Jesus.)

Narrator: Still, Jesus willingly carries the cross he's been given. He is not angry; he doesn't complain. He doesn't even resist. He simply picks up the cross and begins his journey to Calvary.

(Curtains close.)

Narrator: No matter how unfairly Jesus is treated, he willingly picks up the cross and begins the journey that will bring us salvation. Oh, Jesus, your love is so great. Help us to grow in your love!

The Sixth Station

Jesus Meets His Mother

(Characters: Jesus, Mary, soldiers, the crowd, Narrator.)

(Curtains open.)

(Jesus enters stage right, cross resting on shoulder; moving slowly, falters and then regains his balance. Crowd stretches across stage. Mary is among the crowd. Narrator is left of stage.)

Narrator: As Jesus continues his journey, he struggles to balance the weight of the cross. His eyes search the crowd.

(Jesus looks sadly at the crowd as he walks.)

Narrator: Jesus sees people snicker. He sees them sneer.

(Some people in the crowd snicker; some sneer.)

Narrator: He sees people point and whisper.

(Some point and whisper.)

Narrator: But he also sees people crying and praying.

(Some hide faces in hands; some fold hands and bow their heads.)

Narrator: And he sees his mother. Suddenly Jesus stops. His eyes focus on Mary.

(Jesus stops, gazes at Mary; Mary holds her hands to her heart, looks lovingly and sadly at Jesus.)

Narrator: Jesus knows her heart aches. He wishes he could ease her pain. How it hurts him to see his mother so sad! Mary cries for her Son. And she recalls the words that Simeon spoke to her when she and Joseph presented Jesus in the temple when he was young.

(Mary steps forward and recites Simeon's words.)

Mary: "This child is destined to cause the falling and rising of many in Israel, and to be a sign that will be spoken against, so that the thoughts of many hearts will be revealed...."

(Mary wipes her tears and steps back into the crowd.)

Narrator: Like any mother who dearly loves her son—or daughter—Mary wants to protect Jesus from pain. She wishes she could embrace him one more time and tell him how much she loves him, but that isn't possible now. So Mary prays.

Mary: Dear God, help Jesus now.

(Women around Mary hug her as she cries.)

Narrator: Mary also recalls the words the angel spoke to her before Jesus was born.

(Mary looks at the audience.)

Mary: "...You will have a son. His name will be Jesus. He will be great and will be called the Son of God Most High. The Lord God will make him king, as his ancestor David was. He will rule the people of Israel forever, and his kingdom will never end."

Narrator: Mary must wonder what the angel meant by those hopeful words.

(Curtains close.)

Narrator: Sometimes we don't understand why things happen as they do. Sometimes we wonder what God's plans are for our lives. But if we wait and hope, we pray and believe God will help us to understand in time.

The Seventh Station

Jesus Falls

(Characters: Jesus, the crowd, Person #1, Person #2, Person #3, John, soldiers, Narrator.)

(Curtains open.)

(Center stage, Jesus is on the ground with cross lying on his back; soldiers stand nearby; crowd watches, gasps; Narrator stands left of stage.)

Narrator: Jesus hasn't gone far before he stumbles and falls to the ground. He must hear the gasps from the women who watch from a distance. He must know that children turn away or cover their eyes. Jesus prays to his Father.

Jesus: Father, not my will but yours.

(Jesus tries to get up, but the cross holds him down. Soldiers take two steps toward Jesus, and then hold their positions while Narrator delivers his/her lines.)

Narrator: As people in the crowd wait for Jesus to get up, they share memories of Jesus.

(Person #1 steps forward.)

Person #1: I was there the day Jesus healed the man who was lame. He told him to get up, to pick up his mat. And just like that, the man was healed! I tell you, it was a miracle! But why won't he save himself now? I don't understand it.

(Person #1 steps back into crowd.)

(Person #2 steps forward with hands on hips. He frowns and shakes his head.)

Person #2: Hah! The cross is too much for him to bear. Oh, Teacher, look at you now!

(Person #2 steps back into crowd.)

(Person #3 steps toward Jesus.)

Person #3: Some called you "Teacher." They said you were the Messiah. So where are your followers now?

(Person #3 smirks and steps back into the crowd.)

Narrator: Jesus tries to get up. But the cross weighs him down. Mary cries and prays for her son.

(Mary wipes her tears, and then folds her hands.)

Mary: God, how long must this last?

Narrator: Near Mary is John, one of the apostles. He too watches and waits for Jesus to get up. His heart aches for his Teacher and friend. Memories of the past three years rush through John's mind.

(John looks crushed. He shakes his head and closes his eyes; then he steps forward to address the audience.)

John: Don't people know you? Don't they remember all the miracles you have performed? Don't they know who you really are? You could save yourself now, if that's what you wanted. Oh, dear God, help Jesus now.

(Soldiers look irritated, approach Jesus; Jesus gets up and continues walking; crowd becomes animated, talking among themselves.)

Narrator: The soldiers grow tired of waiting for Jesus. They move toward him, but Jesus manages to get up on his own. He is ready to continue his difficult journey.

(Curtains close.)

Narrator: Jesus falls under the weight of this heavy burden, yet he prays for strength to complete this task of love. Let us pray for strength so that we, too, can complete our difficult tasks with love.

The Lent–Easter Book

The Eighth Station

Simon of Cyrene Helps Jesus Carry His Cross

(Characters: Jesus, Soldier #1, Soldier #2, Simon, the crowd, Person #1, Person #2, Person #3, Person #4, Narrator.)

(Curtains open.)

(Center stage: Jesus with cross on shoulder; soldiers to either side; crowd stretches across stage; Narrator left of stage.)

Narrator: The soldiers worry that Jesus won't be able to carry the cross all the way to Calvary. They grow impatient with Jesus' slow-moving steps.

(Both soldiers look irritated. One grabs Jesus' arm to move him along. Soldiers look around. Simon enters stage left, brushing dirt from his hands and clothes, looks around to see what the commotion is about.)

Narrator: One of them sees Simon from Cyrene coming in from the fields. He must have been checking his crops. The soldier thinks Simon looks strong.

(Soldier #1 points at Simon and starts moving in his direction.)

Soldier #1: You, there! Come here! Help carry this cross!

(Simon looks around in disbelief, points to himself, mouthing "Me?")

Soldier #1: Yes, you!

(Simon tries to back away, but the soldier grabs him by the arm, pulling him over to the cross.)

Soldier #2: Come on! Get moving! Pick up that cross!

(Soldiers push Simon toward Jesus.)

Narrator: Simon doesn't have a choice in the matter. The soldiers won't let him refuse. They place the cross on his shoulder.

(One soldier holds Simon's arm, the other places the cross on his shoulder. Simon scowls. People in the crowd look at each other, hands raised in question; they chatter about Simon.)

Person #1: Who is he?

Person #2: I don't know.

Person #3: What did he do?

Person #4: Did he commit a crime, too?

Narrator: Simon's mind races too.

Simon: Why me? What did I do? This isn't fair! People will think I've done something wrong!

(Simon shakes his head and looks at the ground, embarrassed.)

Narrator: Though Simon doesn't understand why he was chosen to help with this task, he carries the cross anyway. He glances at Jesus. Jesus nods at Simon. He's thankful for Simon's help. Suddenly Simon realizes he's helping an innocent man and nothing else matters.

(Simon glances at Jesus; Jesus nods at Simon; all other actors stand motionless and silent.)

(Curtains close.)

Narrator: Sometimes we are asked to do things we'd rather not do. Jesus, help us never to let what others think of us get in our way of helping those in need.

The Ninth Station

Veronica Wipes the Face of Jesus

(Characters: Jesus, Veronica, Simon, soldiers, the crowd, Narrator.)

(Curtains open.)

(Center stage, Jesus with cross on shoulder, Simon behind him, crowd stretched across stage, soldiers on either side of Jesus.)

Narrator: Even though Simon helps Jesus carry his cross, Jesus falters from time to time. The crowd watches, they chatter, they follow his every step. Jesus silently walks on.

(Crowd chatters, then hushes when Jesus falters; soldiers stop and wait to see if he falls; Simon helps balance the cross.)

Narrator: Out of the crowd steps a woman with a veil in her hands. Jesus stops when he sees her approaching.

(Veronica steps forward with veil in hands; Jesus waits for her to approach.)

Narrator: What draws this woman out of the crowd? Does she know Jesus? Does she know his family or friends? Has she heard him preach? Has she heard him speak of the Good Samaritan, the man who stopped to help when no one else would? Does she remember that story as she watches Jesus struggle with his cross? She rushes to him and offers her veil.

(Veronica runs to Jesus, offers her veil; Jesus nods.)

Narrator: Jesus lets her wipe the blood, sweat, and tears from his face. She does this so gently. Jesus appreciates her thoughtfulness.

(Veronica holds the cloth on Jesus' face.)

Narrator: Isn't she afraid that the soldiers will punish her for helping Jesus? Isn't she worried what people will say? Does she know that Jesus is the Teacher, the Son of God? Is that what gives her the courage to step out of the crowd? Suddenly, the soldiers step forward. They push her away from Jesus. Veronica disappears into the crowd.

(Soldiers glare at Veronica; they pull her away from Jesus. She looks over her shoulder at Jesus and then returns to the crowd.)

Narrator: She opens her veil as if to shake dirt from it when she notices the image of Christ's face on the cloth. She bows her head and wipes her tears.

(Veronica opens the veil, sees the image, bows her head, wipes her tears, holds the veil to her heart.)

Narrator: Veronica's simple act of kindness takes only seconds to perform, but her example of compassion will be remembered until the end of the world. Jesus, help us to step out of our crowds of comfort to help others who are hurting. Help us always to care enough to help.

(Curtains close.)

The Lent–Easter Book

The Tenth Station

Jesus Speaks to the Women of Jerusalem

(Characters: Jesus, Simon, Woman #1, Woman #2, Woman #3, women in the crowd, Person #1, the crowd, Soldier #1, Soldier #2, Narrator.)

(Curtains open.)

(Center stage: Jesus and Simon carry the cross, soldiers follow; the crowd watches and talks among themselves; a cluster of women weep and wipe their tears; Narrator stands left of stage.)

Narrator: By now a large crowd is following Jesus. Still, he notices a group of women weeping for him. Other women speak of Jesus.

(Woman #1 steps out of the crowd.)

Woman #1: I was in the crowd the day Jesus cured the crippled woman. She had been crippled for eighteen years. You should have seen her—completely bent over, but when Jesus placed his hands on her and said, "You are now well," she straightened right up and praised God. Jesus is no criminal. He's a healer and teacher. He doesn't deserve this!

(Woman #1 shakes her head and steps back into the crowd.)

(Person #1 steps forward, shakes his finger at Jesus, and delivers his lines.)

Person #1: I was there too. I saw him cure the crippled woman, but he shouldn't have done it on the Sabbath, the day of rest!

(Person #1 steps back into the crowd.)

(Woman #2 steps forward to deliver her lines.)

Woman #2: I was there the day Jesus cured the woman who had been bleeding for years. That's right! She had been bleeding for years. But when she touched Jesus' cloak, she was immediately healed. I tell you, it was a miracle!

(Woman #3 steps forward and faces Woman #2.)

Woman #3: It *was* a miracle! She had been to doctor after doctor, and none of them could heal her. Only Jesus could stop her bleeding.

(Woman #2 and Woman #3 step back into crowd.)

Narrator: Some of these women are mothers with sons of their own. They grieve for Jesus. They grieve for Mary. They know her heart is breaking as she watches her son carry the cross to his death. As Jesus comes near the weeping women, he pauses and speaks to them.

Jesus: Women of Jerusalem, don't cry for me! Cry for yourselves and for your children.

(Women weep even more and wipe their tears.)

Narrator: The soldiers grow impatient.

(Soldiers grab Jesus by the arms and push him forward.)

Soldier #1: We don't have time for this.

Soldier #2: Keep moving! Come on! Move along!

(Jesus turns from the women; he continues moving slowly across the stage.)

Narrator: Jesus turns from the women. He looks forward to the path that leads to our salvation.

(Curtains close.)

Narrator: Out of love and compassion, Jesus, the Teacher, the healer and preacher, takes time to speak with the women. Dear Jesus, our Teacher, please speak to our hearts and help us to learn from you, too.

The Eleventh Station

Jesus Is Nailed to the Cross

(Characters: Jesus, Soldier #1, Soldier #2, the crowd, Person #1, Person #2, Person #3, Person #4, Criminal #1, Criminal #2, Mary, three women, John, Narrator.)

(Curtains open.)

(Left of stage Jesus is nailed to the cross; crowd scattered across rear of stage, watching, talking, praying; soldiers stand guard; two criminals are on crosses to either side of Jesus; Narrator to right of stage.)

Narrator: It's about nine o'clock in the morning. Jesus has just been nailed to the cross. His pain must be unbearable. How can it be that Jesus, the Teacher who had helped and healed so many people, should die like this? Some people in the crowd insult Jesus.

(Jesus grimaces and bows head.)

(Person #1 steps forward to deliver lines.)

Person #1: He saved others, but look, he can't save himself!

(Person #1 shakes head, rolls eyes, and then steps back into crowd.)

(Person #2 and Person #3 step forward to deliver their lines; then step back.)

Person #2: He said he was God's Son!

Person #3: Yeah, right! Let God save him now!

Narrator: But others pray for Jesus.

(Person #4 steps forward with head bowed, hands folded.)

Person #4: Dear God, help Jesus. Have mercy on us all!

(Person #4 steps back.)

(Mary leans on John's shoulder and cries.)

Narrator: John stands by Mary. He tries to comfort her. Then he remembers when Jesus said:

John: "The time has come when you will be scattered. You will go to your homes and leave me alone. But my Father will be with me. I won't be alone. I tell you this that you might have peace."

(John shakes his head as he pats Mary's back.)

Narrator: Right now this is hard for John to understand. What kind of peace makes your heart ache like this? To either side of Jesus, criminals hang on crosses. The one to the right is sorry for what he did; the other is angry.

Criminal #1 (glaring at Jesus): Aren't you the Messiah? Then what are you waiting for? Save yourself! And save us, too!

Narrator: But the criminal to the right of Jesus knows that he and the other criminal deserve their sentences, while Jesus doesn't.

Criminal #2 (glaring at the other criminal): Don't you fear God? Aren't we getting the same punishment as him? We got what was coming to us, but he hasn't done anything wrong.

Narrator: Then he looks to Jesus and asks for forgiveness. And he says:

Criminal #2 (looking at Jesus): Remember me when you come into your Kingdom.

Jesus (looking at Criminal #2 lovingly): I promise that today you will be with me in paradise.

(Criminal simply nods in acknowledgment to Jesus' reply. Jesus nods back.)

(Curtains close.)

Narrator: Dear Jesus, out of love and compassion you forgave the criminal. Please forgive us, too, and help us to forgive others.

The Lent–Easter Book

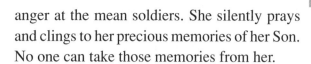

The Twelfth Station

Jesus Speaks to His Mother and the Disciple

(Characters: Jesus, Mary, John, three women, two criminals, two soldiers, small crowd, Narrator.)

(Curtains open.)

(Center stage: Jesus on the cross; smaller crowd is scattered across the rear of the stage, quietly watching; soldiers stand guard; two criminals are on crosses to either side of Jesus; Mary, John, and three women are close to Jesus' cross; Narrator to right of stage.)

Narrator: Mary watches the soldiers divide up her Son's clothes. It must be difficult for her to watch. When it comes to his cloak, they decide not to rip it.

(Soldiers joke, divide clothes, then examine the cloak.)

(Soldier #1 looks at the other soldiers.)

Soldier #1: Let's gamble to see who gets it.

(Soldiers take turns tossing dice, hooting and hollering.)

Narrator: The soldiers do this so the words of Scripture will come true. Scripture says: "They divided up my clothes and gambled for my garments."

Surely Mary would like to keep her Son's cloak. She must be upset at the soldiers' disrespectful behavior, but she doesn't speak out in anger at the mean soldiers. She silently prays and clings to her precious memories of her Son. No one can take those memories from her.

(Soldier #2 smiles and grabs the garment.)

Soldier #2: Ah, hah! It's mine! Give it to me!

(The soldiers return to their posts.)

(Mary, three women, John move closer to the cross. Jesus looks at Mary with compassion.)

Narrator: Jesus is not angry with the soldiers. And he doesn't focus on his own pain. Instead, he is concerned about his heartbroken mother. And he arranges for his dearest apostle to take care of her when he is gone. So Jesus says to his mother:

(Jesus looks from Mary to John.)

Jesus: This man is now your son.

(Jesus looks from John to Mary.)

Narrator: Then Jesus looks from John to Mary and says:

Jesus: She is now your mother.

Narrator: Both Mary and John cry tears of sorrow. They know that Jesus will soon die on the cross. But they know that his love will remain with them always. And their love for him will never fade.

(Mary and John wipe tears from their eyes.)

(Curtains close.)

Narrator: Jesus, the Light of the world, and our way to eternal life, help us to grow in your love.

Reproducible Pages

155

The Thirteenth Station

Jesus Dies on the Cross

(Characters: Jesus, two criminals, soldiers, the crowd, Person #1, Person #2, Person #3, Person #4, Roman Officer, Mary, her friends, John, Narrator.)

(Curtains open.)

(Left of stage, Jesus with head down; criminals with heads down; soldiers walking around crosses; small crowd quiet and to rear of stage; Mary, women, and John kneel near the cross; Narrator to right of stage.)

Narrator: Around noon, the sky darkens. It remains dark until about three o'clock when Jesus cries out:

Jesus (lifting his head and crying out): My God, my God, why have you deserted me?

(Jesus lowers his head.)

Narrator: The crowd is startled.

(Crowd looks surprised.)

Narrator: Some people wonder what Jesus means; others break down and cry. Still others insult him with their remarks.

(Some look puzzled; others wipe their tears.)

(Person #1 steps forward to deliver lines.)

Person #1: He's calling for Elijah. Let's wait and see if Elijah comes to save him!

(Person #1 steps back into the crowd.)

(Person #2 steps forward to deliver lines, then steps back into the crowd.)

Person #2: Let him save himself!

Narrator: Other people in the crowd pray silently for Jesus.

(Some bow in prayer.)

(Person #3 steps forward to deliver line, then steps back.)

Person #3: Dear Father, help him now.

(Person #4 steps forward to deliver line, then steps back.)

Person #4: O God, have mercy on us all.

Narrator: Jesus knows that the time of his death is near. So he says:

Jesus: I am thirsty.

Narrator: He says this so that the words in Scripture will come true. A soldier dips a sponge into a jar of cheap wine and offers it to Jesus.

(A soldier steps out of crowd, dips sponge in a jar, places it on a branch, and raises it to Jesus' mouth.)

Narrator: He drinks the wine and says:

Jesus: Everything is done!

Narrator: Then Jesus says:

Jesus: Father, I put myself into your hands!

(Jesus bows his head.)

(All cast members bow for a moment of silence.)

Narrator: All at once, the ground trembles. A Roman officer says:

Roman officer: This man really was the Son of God!

(Roman officer kneels and bows his head, so do Mary, John, the women, and some of the crowd; others run and exit stage right and left.)

(Curtains close.)

Narrator: No greater love can someone have than to lay down his life for his friends. Jesus, we believe that you are the Son of God and the Savior of the world!

The Lent–Easter Book

The Fourteenth Station

Jesus Is Taken Down from the Cross and Placed in the Tomb

(Characters: Jesus, Mary, three women, John, Joseph from Arimathea, Nicodemus, Person #1, Person #2, soldiers, Pilate, Narrator.)

(Curtains open. A grieving Mary holds Jesus; three women stand behind her, wiping their tears; John kneels to her right; Joseph stands nearby; soldiers stand at a distance; Narrator to the left of stage.)

Mary: Oh, Jesus, sweet Jesus, I love you so much.

(Mary cries, rocks back and forth; the women cry; John pats Mary's back.)

Mary: Dear God, why Jesus? Why now? Please help me. Have mercy on us all.

(Mary wipes her tears; John, Joseph, and women surround Mary in prayer.)

(Curtains close. Everyone but Joseph and Nicodemus exit.)

(Curtains open. Joseph and Nicodemus kneel by Jesus' body.)

Narrator: Joseph from Arimathea has asked permission from Pilate to bury the body. Nicodemus, a Pharisee and Jewish leader, helps Joseph. He remembers the time he asked Jesus:

(Nicodemus turns to audience.)

Nicodemus: How can a man be born again?

Narrator: Nicodemus remembers Jesus' words.

Nicodemus: "You must be born not only of water but of the Spirit, too."

Narrator: Nicodemus has thought about that a lot. Now, he helps to bury the Teacher and healer who taught him so much about faith. As Nicodemus leaves the tomb with Joseph, they roll the stone against the entrance.

(Joseph and Nicodemus roll imaginary stone in front of tomb; exit stage right.)

(Mary Magdalene and Mary, the mother of James, enter stage left and look toward the tomb.)

Narrator: Mary Magdalene and Mary, the mother of James, are watching from a distance.

Mary Magdalene: Let us go and prepare some sweet-smelling spices for the burial.

Narrator: Then the women head for home, planning to anoint Jesus' body after the Sabbath.

(Women exit stage right.)

Narrator: But the women aren't the only ones planning to return to the site. Others visit Pilate the next day to voice their concerns.

(Pilate enters stage right; Person #1 and Person #2 enter stage left and walk over to Pilate.)

Person #1: Sir, this Jesus said in three days he would rise from the dead. We're afraid his followers will steal his body so it looks like he did.

Person #2: Please, Sir, place soldiers outside the tomb so no one can enter.

(Pilate strokes his chin.)

Pilate: Hmmm. All right. Take some soldiers to guard it. And make sure it's tightly sealed.

(Persons #1 and #2 nod and smile.)

Persons #1 and #2: Thank you, Sir! Thank you!

(They exit stage right. Curtains close.)

Narrator: In death as in life, Jesus touched the hearts of others. He came to show us God's love for us, to save us from the power of sin and death, and to give us eternal life. Thank you, Lord Jesus!

The Fifteenth Station

Jesus Rises from the Dead

(Characters: Mary Magdalene; Mary, the mother of James; Salome; Angel.)

(Curtains open.)

(Three women approach the tomb with spices for burial; Angel is sitting inside.)

Narrator: Early Sunday morning, the day after the Sabbath, the women rush to the tomb.

(The women appear to be talking to each other as they hurry to the tomb.)

Mary Magdalene: Who will roll away the stone for us?

Mary, mother of James: Mary! Look! The stone has been rolled away!

(Mary points to tomb; they rush inside, then gasp at what they see.)

Narrator: The women rush inside the tomb. An angel greets them.

(Angel stands near the burial cloths.)

Angel: Do not be afraid. I know you are looking for Jesus.

(Women look wide-eyed at the Angel.)

Salome: Yes, we are looking for Jesus, the Christ, the one they nailed to the cross.

Angel: He isn't here. God has raised him from the dead.

(Women look at each other, confused.)

Angel: See here *(Angel points to his left)*, this is where they placed his body.

(Women look around the tomb; they look at the Angel; they look confused.)

Narrator: The women look around the tomb. Only the burial clothes remain.

Mary Magdalene: But where did he go?

Angel: To Galilee. Now go tell the disciples, especially Peter. Jesus will meet you there.

(The women smile and then rush off to tell the others; exit stage right.)

Narrator: As the Angel said, Jesus meets with his disciples in Galilee. And they all come to believe that he has truly risen from the dead. Amen! Alleluia! Jesus, you are the one who delivered us from slavery into freedom, from darkness into light, from death into life, and who made us a new people. All creation celebrates the resurrection of Christ. Glory to you, Jesus, who rose from the dead! We, too, will live forever with you. Amen. Alleluia!

(Entire cast enters stage from left and right; form two or three lines facing the audience; sing Jesus Christ Is Risen Today.*)*

(Curtains close.)

The Lent–Easter Book

Copyright © 2004, Daughters of St. Paul. All rights reserved. Used with permission.

The Way of the Cross

By Maria Grace Dateno, FSP

Have you ever prayed the Way of the Cross (also called the Stations of the Cross)? You can easily pray this Lenten prayer at your parish church or at a shrine. But how would you like to have to travel over 5,000 miles in order to pray the Way of the Cross?!

Many years ago, people would go to the Holy Land as pilgrims. They wanted to prayerfully follow in the footsteps of Jesus in Jerusalem. They walked along the route that they thought Jesus must have taken as he carried the cross out to the hill of Calvary. The "stations" were the stops along this way, at which they remembered the different episodes of the passion.

However, many people were unable to travel all the way to Jerusalem to retrace the steps of Jesus. People eventually began to set up "stations" in their parish churches. The stations you find in your parish may have pictures on them. Each picture shows something that happened to Jesus on his way to die for us.

The number of stations changed over the years, until the Church settled on the fourteen we know of now. More recently, it has become common to add a fifteenth station: the resurrection. The death and resurrection of Jesus go together. We cannot think of Jesus' death without remembering his resurrection.

The Way of the Cross is a good name for this prayer for two reasons. First, in our heart, we accompany Jesus on his way to Calvary. Secondly, we are reminded that Jesus is always with us on our way through life, especially in times of pain and suffering. This prayer helps us to remember that we are fellow travelers with Jesus.

A good way to pray the Way of the Cross is to imagine that you are walking with Jesus as he carries his cross. If you pray them by yourself, you can walk from station to station. When you pray the Way of the Cross as a group, the leader or the whole group can walk from station to station.

Here are some prayers for praying the Way of the Cross when you are either by yourself or with a group:

Opening Prayer

All: Dear Jesus, who died to save me, I am here to remember your great love for me. I am sorry for the times I have not returned your love. May these Stations of the Cross open my heart more to your gift of love!

If you are with a group, the leader may announce: "The first Station—Jesus is condemned to death."

Leader: We adore you, Jesus, and we praise you.

All: Because by your holy cross you saved the world.

Now say the prayer below the picture of the first station in this book. Repeat these same four steps for each of the other stations.

Closing Prayer

All: Jesus, you love me so much that you were willing to suffer and die on the cross for me. Thank you! Make my love for you and for all my brothers and sisters grow stronger every day. I want to always think, act, and speak as you would. Help me to spread the peace and joy of your resurrection everywhere I go! Amen.

Making Booklets for the Way of the Cross

Make your own mini-book of the Way of the Cross. The Fridays of Lent are a good time to pray this prayer in church or at home. Two reproducible templates for the Way of the Cross are provided: one for primary grades and one for elementary and older grades. When younger children make the Way of the Cross, the teacher or parent can announce each station from the booklet, and the children can respond with the one-line prayer that follows. Provide each child with photocopied pages of the Way of the Cross, and then follow the directions for making the booklet.

Supplies needed:

photocopies of template (primary grades, pages 161–168; older grades, pages 169–170)

scissors

stapler

Directions for Younger Children:

1. Cut out the 4 sets of pages from the side with the tabs.

2. Lay the pages down with all the numbered tabs facing up and the sheet marked "4" on the bottom of the pile.

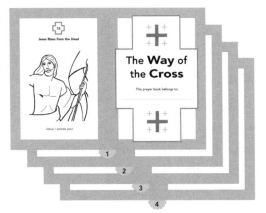

3. Fold the pages in half down the middle so that the cover is on top.

4. Staple your mini-book in the middle and trim off the tabs.

Directions for Older Children:

1. Cut out the 4 sets of pages on the dotted lines.

2. Lay the pages down with all the numbers facing up and the sheet marked "4" on the bottom of the pile.

3. Fold the pages in half down the middle so that the cover is on top.

4. Staple your mini-book in the middle and trim off the tabs.

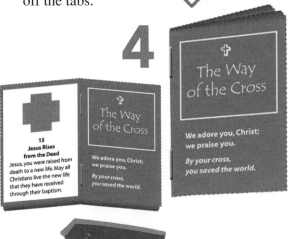

Jesus Rises from the Dead

15

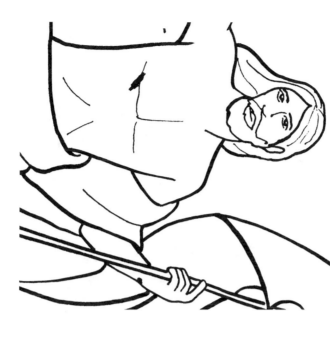

Jesus, I praise you!

The Way of the Cross

This prayer book belongs to:

Jesus Is Laid in the Tomb

14

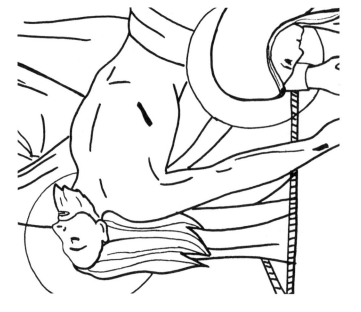

Jesus, have mercy on us.

Jesus Is Condemned to Death

1

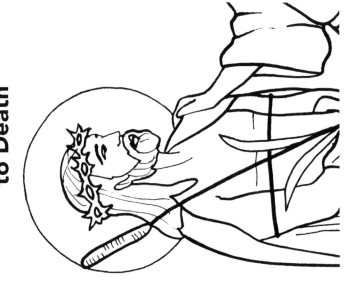

Jesus, I love you.

Jesus Is Taken Down from the Cross

13

Jesus, I love you.

Jesus Carries His Cross

2

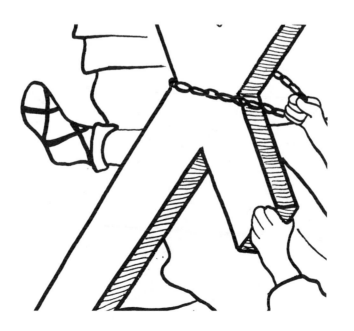

Jesus, I am sad for you.

Jesus Falls the First Time

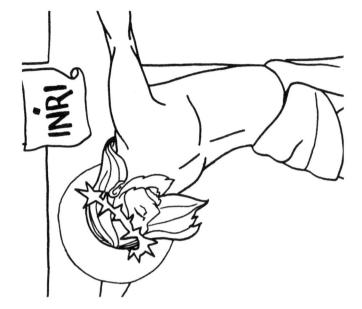

Jesus, I love you.

Jesus Dies on the Cross

12

INRI

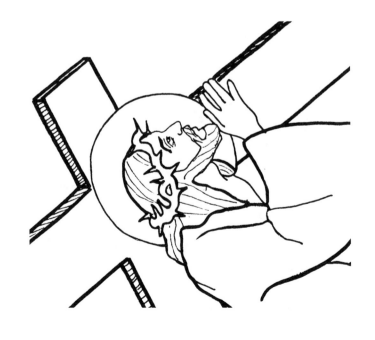

Jesus, thank you.

Jesus Is Nailed to the Cross

11

Jesus, I love you.

Jesus Meets His Mother

4

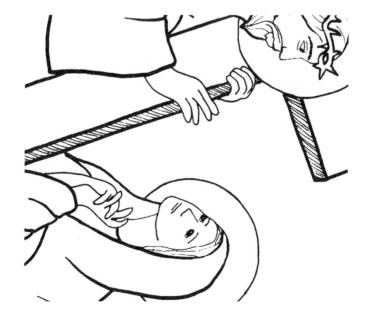

Jesus, I trust you.

3

10
Jesus' Clothes Are Torn Off

Jesus, have mercy on us.

5
Simon of Cyrene Helps Jesus

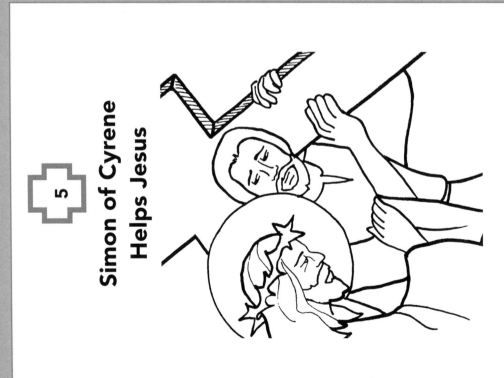

Jesus, I want to help you, too.

Jesus Falls the Third Time

9

Jesus, I want to help you.

Veronica Wipes Jesus' Face

6

Jesus, I love you, too.

4

8
Jesus Meets the Good Women

Jesus, I love you.

7
Jesus Falls the Second Time

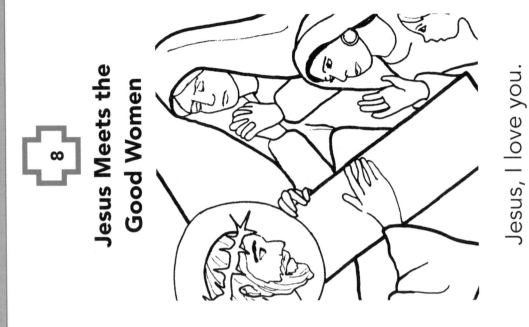

Jesus, have mercy on us.

Jesus Rises from the Dead

15

Jesus, you were raised from death to a new life. May all Christians live the new life that they have received through their baptism.

✝ The Way of the Cross

We adore you, Christ; we praise you.

By your cross you saved the world.

Jesus Is Taken Down from the Cross

13

Jesus, it was very painful for your mother and your friends to see you dead. Please comfort those who are sad because someone they know has died.

Jesus Takes Up His Cross

2

Jesus, you loved us so much that you were willing to carry this heavy cross. Help those who are in pain to remember that you are always with them.

3

Jesus Is Nailed to the Cross

11

Jesus, how much it must have hurt you to be crucified. Please be with all the people who are hurting inside from loneliness or from feeling unloved.

Jesus Meets His Mother

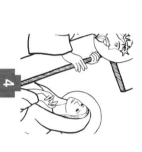

4

Jesus, Mary wanted to be near you, even though it made her sad to see you suffering. Please give me a love that is strong enough to comfort those in my family who are suffering.

Jesus Falls the Third Time

9

Jesus, it must have seemed almost impossible for you to get up and continue on. Please help all people who are addicted to alcohol or drugs to become free from their addiction.

Veronica Wipes Jesus' Face

6

Jesus, Veronica was very brave and kind. She wanted to comfort you, and she did not worry about what people thought of her. I pray for all those who dedicate their time to helping others.

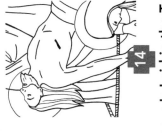

Jesus Is Laid in the Tomb

Jesus, as you were buried in the cave, your friends were afraid that they would never see you again. Help those who live in fear, and let them feel you close to them.

14

Jesus Is Condemned to Death

Jesus, your enemies wanted to kill you, even though you had done nothing wrong. I pray for those who cause others to suffer.

1

Jesus Dies on the Cross

Jesus, as you were dying on the cross, you prayed to your Father, and you thought of us with love. I pray for all those who have died.

12

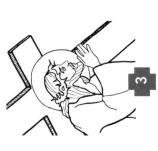

Jesus Falls the First Time

Jesus, it must have been very hard for you to get up after falling. Please be with me when I am having a hard time being good.

3

Jesus' Clothes Are Torn Off

Jesus, how embarrassing this must have been for you. I pray for all those who live in poverty and who are ashamed that they do not have the clothes and food they need.

10

Simon of Cyrene Helps Jesus

Jesus, I think Simon probably did not want to help you at first. Maybe later he was glad he had done it. Help me to use every chance I can to be kind to others.

5

Jesus Meets the Good Women

Jesus, these women were crying for you, in the midst of a crowd that was yelling and laughing at you. I want to pray for all mothers, especially those whose families are having problems.

8

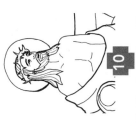

Jesus Falls the Second Time

Jesus, when you fell again, you must have wondered if anyone would help you. Please be with all people who are discouraged and need someone to help them.

7

Name _____

The Blue Ribbon Award

During Lent, we do more penance, pray more often, and make more sacrifices. We do these things as a sign of our love for Jesus and to show sorrow for our sins.

Directions: Find out what the Bible tells us about praying, making sacrifices, and doing penance. Write every other letter found in the Blue Ribbon on the blanks below. Begin with the letter "Y."

Once you've filled in the blanks, unscramble the letters that are circled to find the answer to the statement below. (The letter "C" is used twice.)

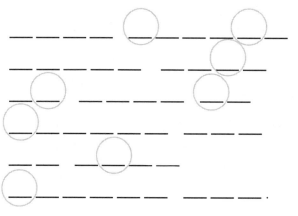

_ _ _ _ _ _

_ _ _ _ _ _

_ _ _ _ _ _

_ _ _ _ _ _ _ _

_ _ _ _ _ _

_ _ _ _ _ _ _ _ _ .

(Matthew 6:4)

During Lent we are called to make

_ _ C _ _ _ _ C _ _ .

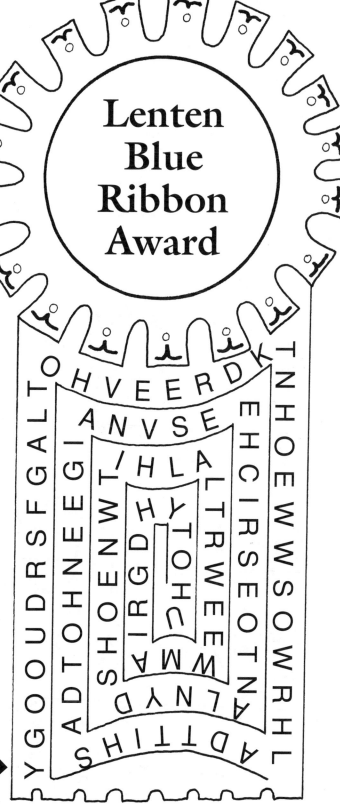

Lenten Blue Ribbon Award

START ▶

Name _____

Prayer Time

During Lent, we spend more time in prayer. Solve the puzzle below to find out how God wants us to pray.

Directions: Choose from the following words: and, God, hearts, prayers, offer, requests, thankful, to, up, with, your. Figure out which words go in which blanks. Then write the words on the blanks and color in the picture below.

W _ _ _   _ _ _ _ _ _ _ _ _   _ _ A _ _ _

_ _ _ _ R   _ _   _ _ _ _   _ _ _ _ _ _ S

_ _ D   _ _ _ _ _ _ _ _ _   _ _   _ _ _ . (Philippians 4:6)

172

The Lent–Easter Book

Name _____

Reconciliation

Jesus taught his disciples to pray. He also taught them how to forgive.

Directions: Follow the arrows and fill in the matching boxes to discover a familiar verse from the Bible that talks about forgiveness (Matthew 6:12).

These words are found in the prayer prayed by Catholics and Christians around the world. Some people call this prayer the

___ ___ ___   ___ ___ ___ ___ ___ ___ ;

others call it the ___ ___ ___ ___ ' ___

___ ___ ___ ___ ___ ___ ___ .

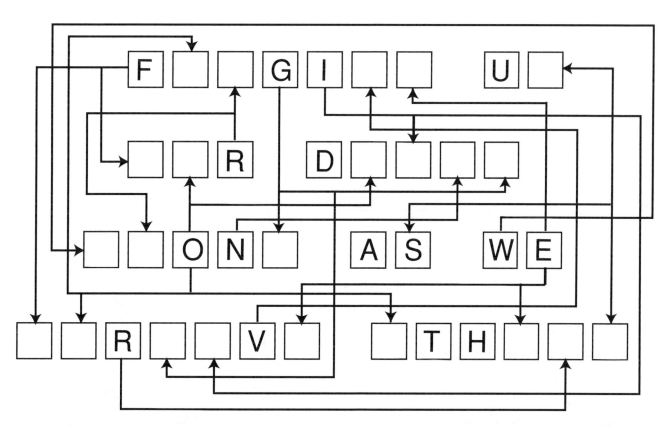

Name _____

Baptism

Directions: Unscramble the letters and write them on the blanks below to find out what
the disciples announced to people of the world. Then color in the picture.

RUNT, ABCK, ZIPTEDAB, MEAN, SEJUS, SCHIRT, ORYU,

NISS, VOEFNRGI, NEHT, OYU, INVEG, YOHL, RIPTIS.

"_ _ _ _   _ _ _ _ _ to God! Be _ _ _ _ _ _ _ _ _

in the _ _ _ _ of _ _ _ _ _   _ _ _ _ _ _ so that

_ _ _ _ _   _ _ _ _ _ will be _ _ _ _ _ _ _ _ _ .

_ _ _ _ _   _ _ _ will be _ _ _ _ _ the _ _ _ _

_ _ _ _ _ _ _ ." *(Acts 2:38)*

The Lent–Easter Book

Name _____

Cross and Resurrection

Jesus told his disciples, "If any of you want to be my followers, you must forget about yourself." But Jesus also told his disciples that they must do something else. And he asks us to do the same (Mark 8:34).

Directions: Find out what Jesus told his disciples by solving the puzzle below. Use the code at the bottom of the page to help you solve the puzzle.

____ ____ ____

____ ____

____ ____ ____ ____ ____ ____ ____ ____ .

Cross Code:

A	C	D	E	F	K	L	M	N	O	P	R	S	T	U	W	Y

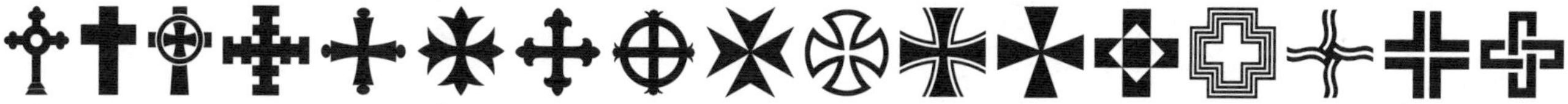

Do you have a "cross" to carry? Something that is difficult for you to do? Ask Jesus to help you carry your "cross." Then on the back of this paper, draw a picture of your "cross" or write a prayer asking Jesus to help you carry your "cross."

Name _____

The Bread of Life

Directions: Find out what Jesus told his disciples about the Bread of Life by solving the puzzle below. Match the pieces to their place on the puzzle. Then write the words in order clockwise on the line provided. When you're finished, color in the puzzle.

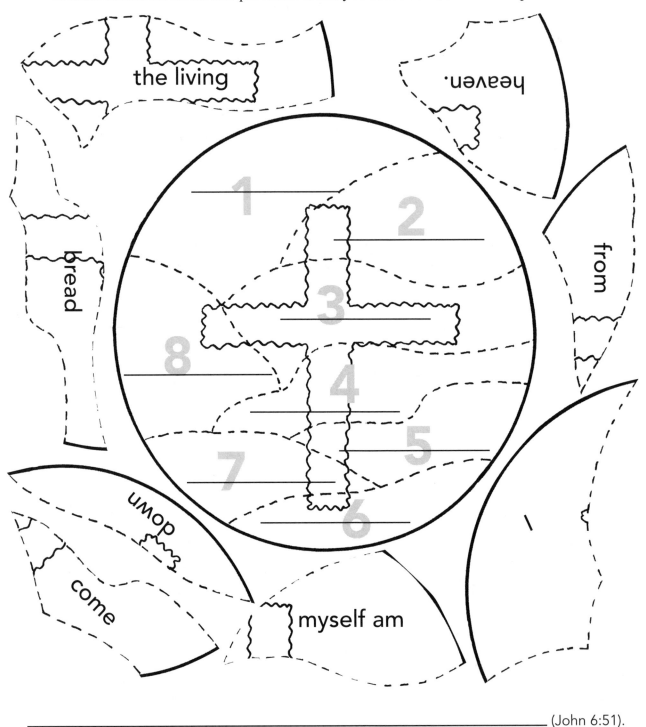

_____ (John 6:51).

176

The Lent–Easter Book

Name _____

The New Command

After Jesus shared the Last Supper with his apostles, he gave them a new command. Do you know what he said? (John 13:34) Find out by solving the puzzle.

Directions: Use the code below to help you solve the puzzle.

___ ___ ___   ___ ___ ___   ___ ___ ___ ___

___ ___ ___ ___   ___ ___ ___ ___ ___   ___ ___ ___ ___ ___ ___

___ ___   ___ ___ ___ ___ ___   ___ ___ ___ ___ ___ ___ ___   ___ ___ ___ .

Hearts Code:

| A | C | D | E | H | I | J | L | M | O | R | S | T | U | V | Y |

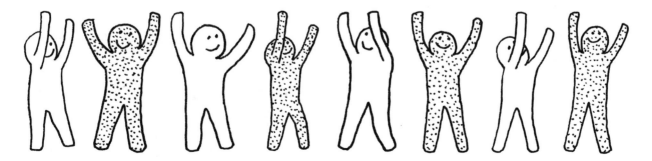

Name _____

Easter

Jesus is risen! Alleluia! The word alleluia means "Glory to God!"

Directions: Unscramble the words and fill in the blanks to complete the story of Easter. Then color in the picture and share the Easter story with your family and friends.

Very early Sunday morning, Mary Magdalene and some of her friends went to the tomb where Jesus had been buried. The women were frightened because the stone had been rolled away from the tomb. An angel greeted them and told them...

Do not be (1) __ __ __ __ __ __ . You are (2) __ __ __ __ __ __ __
for (3) __ __ __ __ __ from (4) __ __ __ __ __ __ __ __ who
was (5) __ __ __ __ __ __ to the (6) __ __ __ __ __ . He is
(7) __ __ __ (8) __ __ __ __ . He is (9) __ __ __ __ __ . Go tell his
(10) __ __ __ __ __ __ __ __ __ that he will meet them in
(11) __ __ __ __ __ __ __ *(Mark 16:6–7).* And he did.

(1) IFADRA	(7) TON	
(2) KNOOLGI	(8) EHER	
(3) SUEJS	(9) SREIN	
(4) AZNAHRTE	(10) SLEIPDISC	
(5) LIADEN	(11) LEAGLIE	
(6) SCROS		

The Lent–Easter Book

Name _____

Ascension

Directions: Solve the puzzle below to find out what Jesus told his disciples before he ascended into heaven.

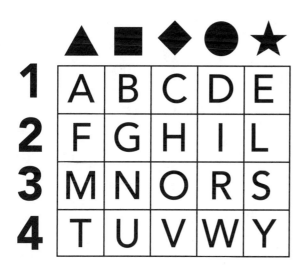

Matthew 28:20

2-● 4-● 2-● 2-★ 2-★ 1-■ 1-★

— — — — — — —

4-● 2-● 4-▲ 2-◆ 4-★ 3-◆ 4-■

— — — — — — —

1-▲ 2-★ 4-● 1-▲ 4-★ 3-★, 1-★ 4-◆ 1-★ 3-■

— — — — — —, — — — —

4-■ 3-■ 4-▲ 2-● 2-★ 4-▲ 2-◆ 1-★ 1-★ 3-■ 1-●

— — — — — — — — — — —

3-◆ 2-▲ 4-▲ 2-◆ 1-★ 4-● 3-◆ 3-● 2-★ 1-●.

— — — — — — — — — —.

Name _____

Gifts of the Spirit

The Holy Spirit blesses each of us with different gifts. And we share these gifts with others.

Directions: See how many "gifts" you can find in the word search.

Created with Discovery Channel School's PuzzleMaker.

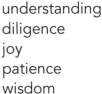

```
E S V T V Y T H E A G N S U U
C W S M O S T G T O V S B N G
N O U E U L D I O I E V D N C
E W U R N E E D T N A E R O G
I K T N L E N R D S R F U I H
T L J W S E L N A S A R B S O
A W O O S E I T T N A H Q S L
P N V S Y K L A N G C H C A I
K L O V E I N U E E Z E D P N
E S S E N D L I M D G R Q M E
C D I L I G E N C E G V Y O S
A E C N A R E V E S R E P C S
E B G M O D E S T Y M R Z B L
P Y T I R A H C E M P A T H Y
M O D S I W H D Y C T R P H X
```

charity
empathy
kindness
peace
chastity
faith
knowledge
perseverance
compassion
gentleness
love
tolerance
counsel
goodness
mildness
trust
courage
holiness
modesty
understanding
diligence
joy
patience
wisdom

Write some of the "gifts" you can share with others in the packages below.

The Lent–Easter Book

Name _____

Teach Me to Follow

During the Easter season, we celebrate our gift of new life in Jesus.

Directions: Find the path that leads from beginning to end, and then color in the butterfly, a symbol of new life.

Show me your paths and teach me to follow, guide me by your truth and instruct me.

(Psalm 25:4–5)

ANSWERS

Page 171

Your Father knows what is done in secret and he will reward you. Sacrifices.

Page 172

With thankful hearts offer up your prayers and requests to God.

Page 173

Our Father; Lord's Prayer.

Forgive us for doing wrong as we forgive others.

Page 174

Turn back to God. Be baptized in the name of Jesus Christ so that your sins will be forgiven. Then you will be given the Holy Spirit.

Page 175

Take up your cross and follow me.

Page 176

I myself am the living bread come down from heaven.

Page 177

You must love each other, just as I have loved you.

Page 178

Do not be afraid. You are looking for Jesus from Nazareth, who was nailed to the cross. He is not here. He is risen. Go tell his disciples that he will meet them in Galilee.

Page 179

I will be with you always, even until the end of the world.

Page 180

```
E S V T V Y T H E A G N S U U
C W S M O S T G T O V S B N G
N O U E U L D I O I E V D N C
E W U R N E E D T N A E R O G
I K T N L E N R D S R F U I H
T L J W S E L N A S A R B S O
A W O O S E I T T N A H Q S L
P N V S Y K L A N G C H C A I
K L O V E I N U E E Z E D P N
E S S E N D L I M D G R Q M E
C D I L I G E N C E G V Y O S
A E C N A R E V E S R E P C S
E B G M O D E S T Y M R Z B L
P Y T I R A H C E M P A T H Y
M O D S I W H D Y C T R P H X
```

Page 181

The Advent–Christmas Book

BOOKS & MEDIA

The Daughters of St. Paul operate book and media centers at the following addresses. Visit, call or write the one nearest you today, or find us on the World Wide Web, www.pauline.org

CALIFORNIA
3908 Sepulveda Blvd, Culver City, CA 90230 — 310-397-8676
2650 Broadway Street, Redwood City, CA 94063 — 650-369-4230
5945 Balboa Avenue, San Diego, CA 92111 — 858-565-9181

FLORIDA
145 S.W. 107th Avenue, Miami, FL 33174 — 305-559-6715

HAWAII
1143 Bishop Street, Honolulu, HI 96813 — 808-521-2731
Neighbor Islands call: — 866-521-2731

ILLINOIS
172 North Michigan Avenue, Chicago, IL 60601 — 312-346-4228

LOUISIANA
4403 Veterans Memorial Blvd, Metairie, LA 70006 — 504-887-7631

MASSACHUSETTS
885 Providence Hwy, Dedham, MA 02026 — 781-326-5385

MISSOURI
9804 Watson Road, St. Louis, MO 63126 — 314-965-3512

NEW JERSEY
561 U.S. Route 1, Wick Plaza, Edison, NJ 08817 — 732-572-1200

NEW YORK
64 W. 38th Street, New York, NY 10018 — 212-754-1110

PENNSYLVANIA
9171-A Roosevelt Blvd, Philadelphia, PA 19114 — 215-676-9494

SOUTH CAROLINA
243 King Street, Charleston, SC 29401 — 843-577-0175

VIRGINIA
1025 King Street, Alexandria, VA 22314 — 703-549-3806

CANADA
3022 Dufferin Street, Toronto, Ontario, Canada M6B 3T5 — 416-781-9131

¡También somos su fuente para libros, videos y música en español!